SRA
Reading
Success

Effective Comprehension Strategies

Student Workbook

Level
C

Mc
Graw
Hill **SRA**

Columbus, OH

SRAonline.com

 SRA

ISBN: 978-0-07-618483-5
MHID: 0-07-618483-8

1 2 3 4 5 6 7 8 9 MAL 13 12 11 10 09 08 07

The **McGraw·Hill** Companies

Lesson 1

Part A - Pronouns

You probably know that pronouns refer to people or things. A person named Sojourner Truth is referred to 12 times in the passage below, counting her name and the pronouns she, her, and hers that refer to her.

Sojourner Truth was born into slavery in New York in 1795. She gained her freedom in 1827, when the state freed its slaves. After working as a servant for several years, she became a public speaker on behalf of abolition and the rights of women.

In 1851, she attended a women's convention in Akron, Ohio. Other people attending the convention did not support the attendance of a freed slave. They were afraid that their cause, the rights of women, would be damaged if it were associated with the right of blacks.

When the president of the convention introduced her, she was met with hisses. Sojourner Truth rose from her seat and made her way to the platform. People say that when Sojourner Truth began speaking, her vivid, moving words had a "magical" effect on everyone at the convention.

Some of the most common pronouns are: I, me, you, we, she, her, hers, it, its, they, them, their, and theirs.

Part B - Pronouns

Directions: Read the paragraph below. Underline every time Frederick Douglass is referred to. Then fill in the blank to show how many times Frederick Douglass is referred to.
HINT: Look for the pronouns he, him, and his.

Frederick Douglass was born a slave in Maryland in 1817. In the South before the Civil War, it was against the law for him to learn to read and write. But those who were determined, including Douglass, managed to learn.

While in slavery, he worked as a house servant, a field hand, and a ship carpenter. When he was twenty-one, he escaped from slavery and made his way to Massachusetts. In time, he joined the antislavery movement and became a powerful speech maker.

In 1845, he became the author of a book about his years in slavery. The title of his book was *Narrative of the Life of Frederick Douglass.* The book made him famous. The laws at the time said that an escaped slave living in a free state could be caught and returned to his owner. To avoid being recognized and captured, Douglass left America to give speeches in England. When he returned to America, he bought his freedom. At that time, Douglass started an antislavery newspaper. During the Civil War, <u>he</u> recruited African-Americans for the Union Army. Shortly before his death, he became the United States' ambassador to Haiti.

1. How many times is Frederick Douglass referred to in the paragraph above, counting both his name and the pronouns that refer to him?

Part C- Literal Questions

The most basic type of question to ask yourself when you read is a **literal** question. The answer to a **literal** question is found in the passage.

Example: Read the passage below, paying special attention to the underlined part. Then, read the **literal** question below the passage.

<u>A Winter Feast will be held from 6 to 8 p.m. at the Hollow Inn Grange, 110 11th Ave. S.E.</u> The third annual event includes a vegetarian dinner and music. Local eateries will donate food for the feast, but guests should also bring their favorite vegetarian dish to share. Donations will be $4 for students and seniors, and $5 for adults. All donations will support the restoration of the Hollow Inn Grange Hall.

Here is a **literal** question about the underlined part:
At what time will the Winter Feast be held?

There are different ways to write the answer from the passage:
6 to 8 pm
six to eight o'clock in the evening
6 to 8 at night

Part D- Literal Questions

Directions: Read the passage below. Then answer the literal questions. NOTE: There are TWO correct answers to each question.

Smoky exhaust from cars and factories that burn fossil fuels can damage the environment. This is a serious problem because most of the world's energy is provided by coal, oil, and natural gas.

Because of these concerns, people have been motivated to search for new energy sources. For example, thousands of windmills provide the city of San Francisco, California, with some of its electrical power. Located in California's Mojave Dessert is the world's largest solar energy plant. This plant furnishes some of the electricity needed by the city of Los Angeles, California. Mirrors focus the sunlight on tubes of mineral oil. The oil gets hot enough to boil water. The steam that is produced powers the generators.

The sun and wind have long been used as power sources. They are not the final solutions to the world's energy needs, though. What happens if the wind doesn't blow and the sun doesn't shine?

Mark the TWO correct answers to each question.

1. According to the article, which two cities in California get part of their electrical power from sources other than fossil fuels?

    a. Oakland

    b. San Francisco

    c. San Diego

    d. Los Angeles

2. The two alternative power sources mentioned in the article are:

    a. water

    b. wood

    c. wind

    d. sun

3. What are two examples of fossil fuels mentioned in the passage?

   a. hydrogen gas

   b. coal

   c. oil

   d. nuclear

Part E- Bonus

The bonus word for this lesson is **anaphora**.

Anaphora is pronounced like this:

   uh•NA•for•uh

Anaphora means "a pronoun or other words used to refer to some other word or name." When you use **anaphora**, you avoid repeating the same word over and over again.

We have been using **anaphora** in this lesson. Pronouns are one type of **anaphora**. For example, above in Part B when the author used the word "he" in the place of "Frederick Douglass," the author was using **anaphora**.

Anaphora will be a bonus item on some quizzes or tests that you take.

Anaphora comes from the Greek language. *Ana* means "up" and *pherein* means "carry" in Greek. So anaphora "carries you up" (or refers back) to a previously mentioned word.

To learn **anaphora**, you will have to know what it means, how to spell it, and where it comes from.

Optional Prosody Exercise

Part F - Reading Aloud

Directions: Listen to your teacher read the sentences below. Your teacher will read them so that they sound like normal English when it is spoken. If your teacher calls on you to read one of the sentences, try to read it so that it sounds like someone speaking. Take your time. You can read the sentence silently before reading it aloud.

1. The steam that is produced powers the generators.

2. Local eateries will donate food for the feast, but guests should also bring their favorite vegetarian dish to share.

3. What are two examples of fossil fuels mentioned in the passage?

4. So anaphora "carries you up" (or refers back) to a previously mentioned word.

Lesson 2

Part A - Pronouns

Directions: Read the paragraph below. Underline every time "the parade" is referred to. Then fill in the blank to show how many times "the parade" is referred to.
HINT: Look for the pronouns it and its.

I had never seen such a fine parade. It started out with a fabulous horse patrol followed by flags and banners that looked like a moving rainbow. The parade's spectators "oohed and aahed" as the floats slowly made their way along the parade route. Its announcer could barely be heard above the noise of all the marching bands. The judges' stand was located high enough over the parade so that they could see its beauty from beginning to end. The grand marshal of the parade rode in a red convertible and threw candy to the crowd. The fire trucks brought up the rear of the parade, complete with a dalamation riding in the front seat! As icing on the cake, the setting sun put on a spectacular show as the parade snaked its way to the fairgrounds.

How many times is "the parade" referred to in the paragraph above, counting both the word and pronouns that refer to it?

Part B- Literal Questions

Directions: Read the passage below. Then answer the literal questions. NOTE: There are TWO correct answers to each question.

You've just gotten into a television program, and the next thing you know, you can't find it on its regular channel at its regular time. In fact, you can't find it anywhere. What happened to it? It was probably cancelled and replaced with another program. How can this happen, and who is responsible?

The answer to that question is television ratings. Television ratings try to estimate how many people are watching various television programs. Television programs with high ratings can charge advertisers more money to run commercials than less popular shows can. Because most television stations rely on advertising to pay for their costs, low-rated programs usually get cancelled.

How are the television ratings determined? Companies provide rating services that survey a sample of American families who own television sets. An electronic measuring device called the "people meter" is installed in each home taking part in the survey. A rating is determined by the number of homes taking part in the survey that have their television sets tuned to a particular program. So, if your favorite show has been cancelled, chances are good that people taking part in the survey didn't like the show as much as you did!

Mark the TWO correct answers to each question.

1. What things are most important to a television station?

    a.   station location

    b.   name of station

    c.   ratings

    d.   number of advertisers

2. How do television stations determine ratings?

    a.   by surveying a sample of American families with televisions

    b.   surprise visits to people's homes to see what they're watching at the time

    c.   surveys sent out in the mail to all American families

    d.   by installing electronic "people meters"

3. According to the article, which statements are true?

    a.   A television show with a high rating can charge advertisers more money to run their commercials.

    b.   At one time or another, every home with a television will take part in the ratings survey.

    c.   Television shows can be cancelled because of poor ratings.

    d.   A television show with a poor rating can be moved to another time or day to increase its ratings.

Part C - Inference

When you read something, you can ask yourself questions that are not directly answered in the passage you are reading. For example, how do you think Buster's family feels in the passage below?

On Saturday, posters appeared everywhere in our neighborhood. They were on the mailboxes, on our doors, and even in the window of the neighborhood grocery store. "Buster," a german shepherd who belonged to a family living a few blocks over, had disappeared. The family hadn't seen him for about a week. According to the poster, the family was even offering a reward to anyone who could find him.

If you've lost something that means a great deal to you, and you can't find it, you would probably feel *very worried or desperate.*

Part D - Inference

Directions: Read the passage below. Think about how Tim and his friends feel in the passage, and then answer the question below.

Tim and his friends, Joe and Kate, saw the posters and decided to launch "Operation Find Buster." First, they told their parents what they had in mind, and got their permission. Then, they packed some water, some snacks, and some doggie treats in case they found Buster. The group got on their bikes and began to search the neighborhood for Buster. Early in the afternoon, they found Buster walking along the railroad tracks at the edge of town. They returned him to his family. The family was overjoyed to see Buster, who was hungry, but safe and sound. Tim and his friends had agreed ahead of time that they wouldn't accept the reward money, even though they were all saving for something special.

1. When Tim and his friends returned Buster and didn't accept the reward, how do you think they felt?
    a. dishonest
    b. selfish
    c. proud
    d. clever

Part E- Bonus

Anaphora will be a bonus item on some quizzes or tests that you take.

Anaphora means "a pronoun or other words used to refer to some other word or name." When you use **anaphora**, you avoid repeating the same word or name over and over again.

Anaphora comes from the Greek words that mean "up" and "carry."

To learn **anaphora**, you will have to know what it means, how to spell it, and where it comes from.

Optional Prosody Exercise

Part F - Reading Aloud

Directions: Listen to your teacher read the sentences below. Your teacher will read them so that they sound like normal English when it is spoken. If your teacher calls on you to read one of the sentences, try to read it so that it sounds like someone speaking. Take your time. You can read the sentence silently before reading it aloud.

1. When you read something, you can ask yourself questions that are not directly answered in the passage you are reading.

2. According to the article, which statements are true?

3. At one time or another, every home with a television will take part in the ratings survey.

4. When Tim and his friends returned Buster and didn't accept the reward, how do you think they felt?

Lesson 3

Part A- Anaphora

You know that pronouns are a type of **anaphora**. They refer to a noun or a noun phrase.

Sometimes, other kinds of words also refer to a noun or a noun phrase.

Let's say we're talking about the sun. In addition to using a pronoun such as "it," we could also refer to the sun as:

the giant sphere of fire

great ball of gas

the massive glowing orb

the star

Sol

These are all ways we could refer to the sun. These ways are examples of **anaphora**.

Part B- Anaphora

Directions: Read the paragraph below. Underline every reference to bats. That is, underline every use of the word bat, or pronouns or other words that mean bat.

You may be surprised to know that stars aren't only visible at night. In fact, there's one you can only see during the day . . . the sun! That's right, the sun is a star. The giant sphere of fire we wake up to is nothing more than a great ball of gas held together by its own gravity. It is sometimes referred to by its Latin name, *Sol*, which is where the name Solar System comes from: the Solar System is the matter (including the Earth and other planets, meteoroids and comets) that orbits the sun. The massive glowing orb alone accounts for more than 99% of the Solar System's mass. Energy from the star supports almost all life on Earth through photosynthesis and drives the Earth's climate and weather.

1. Who or what is talked about the most in this paragraph?

_____

2. About how many times is the sun talked about in the paragraph?

_____

Remember, if you use other words in addition to pronouns to refer to someone or something when you write, that will make your writing better. For example, if you call the sun not only by its name, but also by pronouns like "it" and by phrases like "the massive glowing orb," your writing will be more interesting.

Part C - Inference

Directions: Read the passage below. Think about how Peter feels in the passage, and then answer the question below.

It was the first day of camp for Peter. Four boys were assigned to each cabin, and Peter had arrived a day late. The other three boys had already chosen their bunks, gotten to know each other, and signed up for their favorite activities. As Peter was unpacking, the three other boys burst through the door laughing and playfully shoving each other around. As soon as they saw Peter, they stopped in their tracks and suddenly became quiet.

1. How do you think Peter probably felt when his cabin mates arrived?

     a.   nervous

     b.   angry

     c.   surprised

     d.   fine

Part D- Classification

You probably know how to classify things. For example, the following items belong to one class of things:

menu, waiter or waitress, reservation, doggie bag, free refills

To classify, you must decide what all of those things have in common. In this case, all of the things belong to the class of "going out to eat."

Many times, being able to classify well helps you better understand what you read. Classifying also helps you when you write.

Part E- Classification

Directions: After reading each list below, classify the items in the list.

1. knowing emergency phone numbers
   having a good sense of responsibility
   knowledge of basic first aid
   liking children

   These are all things that are important when someone is going to be:

   _____

2. roller coasters
   standing in long lines
   feeling dizzy or queasy
   dealing with crowds
   eating junk food
   winning prizes

   These are all things someone might do when:

   _____

3. computer
   dictionary
   thesaurus
   pencils and paper
   encyclopedias
   books, videos, and CDs
   highlighter

   These are all things someone might need for:

   _____

Part F- Bonus

Anaphora will be a bonus item on some quizzes or tests that you take.

Anaphora means "a pronoun or other words used to refer to some other word or name." When you use **anaphora**, you avoid repeating the same word or name over and over again.

Anaphora comes from the Greek words that mean "up" and "carry."

To learn **anaphora**, you will have to know what it means, how to spell it, and where it comes from.

Optional Prosody Exercise

Part G - Reading Aloud

Directions: Listen to your teacher read the sentences below. If your teacher calls on you to read one of the sentences, try to read it so that it sounds like someone speaking. Take your time. You can read the sentence silently before reading it aloud.

1. About how many times is the sun talked about in the paragraph?

2. After reading each list below, classify the items in the list.

3. How do you think Peter probably felt when his cabin mates arrived?

4. **Anaphora** comes from the Greek words that mean "up" and "carry."

Lesson 4

Part A- Anaphora

Directions: Read the paragraph below. Underline every reference to "volcanoes." That is, underline every use of the name, or pronoun, or other words that mean "volcanoes."

There are three different causes of volcanoes. Those violent occurrences can occur as the result of plates in the earth's crust pressing in against each other. They can also result from those plates moving away from each other, creating an opening for the hot molten material under the earth's crust to come through. Many people know that volcanoes can be caused by hot spots in the earth's crust. Those often result in the formation of large mountains. However they are caused, most of us are fascinated by these natural wonders.

1. Who or what is talked about the most in this paragraph?

_____

2. How many times are volcanoes referred to in the paragraph?

_____

Remember, if you use other words in addition to pronouns to refer to someone or something when you write, that will make your writing better. For example, if you call "volcanoes" not only by their name, but also by pronouns like "they" and by phrases like "these natural wonders," your writing will be more interesting.

Part B- Literal Questions

Directions: Read the paragraph below. Then answer the literal questions. NOTE: There are TWO correct answers to each question.

Ballads tell a dramatic story using verses or stanzas. Early ballads were sung or recited by wandering minstrels. Each generation of minstrels remembered the basic outline of the ballads, but often used the popular figures of the day as main characters.

Perhaps the most famous figure in ballads is Robin Hood. Robin Hood lived in Sherwood Forest in England with his band of merry men. Robin Hood was an outlaw, but he was a friend of poor and mistreated people. The character of Robin Hood first appeared in English ballads in the 1300's. Figures of American ballads include the outlaw Jesse James, the railroad engineer Casey Jones, and "mighty" Casey, a baseball player.

Mark the TWO correct answers to each question.

1. According to the passage, in what two ways were ballads spread?

    a.   sung

    b.   heard on the radio

    c.   written

    d.   recited

2. Robin Hood was a friend of:

    a.   the rich

    b.   the mistreated

    c.   the poor

    d.   the King and Queen of England

3. Which two topics of ballads are listed in the passage?

    a.   The Three Musketeers

    b.   Robin Hood

    c.   Billy the Kid

    d.   Casey Jones

Part C- Classification

Directions: After reading each list below, classify the items in the list.

1. uniforms

   musicians

   rehearsal

   performance

   conductor

   audience

   instruments

   These are all a part of being in:

_____

2. playing basketball

   riding a bike

   swimming

   playing volleyball

   ballet

   running

   walking

   roller blading

   These are all types of:

_____

3. Mt. Rushmore
   Old Faithful
   Lincoln Memorial
   Vietnam Memorial
   Golden Gate Bridge
   Custer's Last Stand
   The Alamo

   These are all:

Part D- Bonus

Remember, **anaphora** will be a bonus item on some quizzes or tests that you take.

Anaphora means "a pronoun or other words used to refer to some other word or name." When you use **anaphora**, you avoid repeating the same word or name over and over again.

Anaphora comes from the Greek words that mean "up" and "carry."

To learn **anaphora**, you will have to know what it means, how to spell it, and where it comes from.

Optional Prosody Exercise

Part E - Reading Aloud

Directions: Listen to your teacher read the sentences below. If your teacher calls on you to read one of the sentences, try to read it so that it sounds like someone speaking. Take your time. You can read the sentence silently before reading it aloud.

1. Each generation of minstrels remembered the basic outline of the ballads, but often used the popular figures of the day as main characters.

2. Which two topics of ballads are listed in the passage?

3. Ballads tell a dramatic story using verses or stanzas.

4. How many times are volcanoes referred to in the paragraph?

Lesson 5

Optional Prosody Exercise

Directions: Listen to your teacher read the sentences below. If your teacher calls on you to read one of the sentences, try to read it so that it sounds like someone speaking. Take your time. You can read the sentence silently before reading it aloud.

1. What **TWO** things are referred to, along with the earth, as the giver of life?

2. That is, underline every use of the name, or pronouns or other words that refer to "the planet earth."

3. Humans belong to what class of vertebrates?

4. It is possible, however, for us humans to damage the atmosphere around <u>our home</u>.

Lesson 6

Part A - Anaphora

Directions: Read the paragraph below. Underline every reference to "snowflakes." That is, underline every time "snowflakes" are referred to in the passage, either by name, by pronouns, or by other words.

Snowflakes have a delicate six-pointed shape. All are different from each other. You would need a microscope to see their elaborate patterns. These white puffs begin their short lives when an ice crystal forms around a speck of dust or other matter. They grow as they pick up more ice crystals. As the snowflakes become heavier, they begin to fall. On their way to the ground, they go through many changes as the result of changes in the temperature and moisture content of the air. These changes affect their growth pattern. These enchanting stars each take a different path to the ground, so they each meet slightly different conditions. That's why no two snowflakes look exactly alike.

In very cold air, lacy stars with sharp tips are formed. In warmer air, the flakes may become flat, six-sided plates or needle-like crystals. If the air is warmer still, snowflakes clump together.

When snowflakes reach the ground, they will change their shape. If temperatures are warm, they melt. Even if snowflakes don't melt, they quickly change into tiny, smooth-sided grains. To see these delicate beauties, you need to look closely--and quickly!

1. Who or what is talked about most in this paragraph?

_____

2. How many times are snowflakes mentioned?

_____

Part B - Anaphora and Classification

Directions: Classify these details from the above passage.

delicate six-pointed
lacy stars with sharp tips
flat, six-sided plates
needle-like crystals
tiny, smooth-sided grains
delicate beauties
ice crystal forms around a speck of dust

These phrases all suggest that snowflakes:

_____

Part C- Inference

Directions: Read the paragraph below and then answer the questions.

Have you ever been "picked on"? If you have, you're not alone. In a survey, almost one out of every three students in grades six through ten said that they were involved in bullying. They were either victims, doing the bullying, or both. Both girls and boys are involved in bullying.

Bullying is a serious problem. Concern about it has been growing recently because it has been linked to some terrible incidents of school violence. Do you know what to do if you or someone you know is being bullied? Many schools are taking action to put an end to bullying.

Here are some steps you can take that may be helpful:

1. If you see someone being bullied, stand up for the victim. Tell the bully to stop.

2. If you're the victim of bullying, tell your parents what's going on at school. They can talk to your teachers or counselors at school, or they can talk to the bully's parents.

3. Talk to teachers or counselors about bullying that you see or might experience. They can help put a stop to it before it goes too far.

1. How do you think a person feels who is being bullied?

_____

2. Why do you think a person would bully someone else?

_____

_____

Part D - Bonus

The bonus word for this lesson is **literal**.

Literal is pronounced like this:

LIT•er•ul

Literal comes from the Latin word *littera* (LIT er ah), which means "letter" or "word."

When you take a reading test, some of the questions you have to answer are **literal questions**. That means that you can find the answer to the questions in the passage you are reading.

To learn **literal**, you will have to know what it means, where it comes from, and how to spell it.

Part E- Bonus

Another bonus word for this lesson is **inference**.

Inference is pronounced like this:

IN•fur•unse

Inference means "guessing about something from another thing that you already know." You inferred a bullying victim's feelings in the above passage, even though the passage doesn't tell you directly how that victim feels.

To learn **inference,** you will have to know what it means and how to spell it.

Optional Prosody Exercise

Part F - Reading Aloud

Directions: Listen to your teacher read the sentences below. If your teacher calls on you to read one of the sentences, try to read it so that it sounds like someone speaking. Take your time. You can read the sentence silently before reading it aloud.

1. How do you think a person feels who is being bullied?

2. **Inference** means "guessing about something from another thing that you already know."

3. Many schools are taking action to put an end to bullying.

Lesson 7

Part A - Main Idea

In this lesson, you are going to combine everything you have learned about anaphora and classifying. By combining these skills, you will learn to determine the main idea of a passage. A main idea is like a summary.

Part B - Main Idea

Directions: Read the paragraph below. Decide who or what is talked about most and classify the details from the passage.

HINT: If you are not sure, read the passage once and take a guess. Then underline all the references to what you have guessed. That way you will be able to see how many times that person or thing is mentioned.

A modern symphony orchestra may include more than 100 musicians, playing many different musical instruments. There are four major sections in an orchestra: stringed instruments, woodwind instruments, brass instruments, and percussion instruments. Each group is seated in sections according to a traditional plan.

The percussion section is in the back. The kettledrums are the stars there. Other drums, and just about anything else that makes a sound when it's hit or shaken, may be part of the percussion section.

On the right and left of the conductor are the violins. There are usually 30 or more. Violins are the smallest of the stringed instruments. They are joined by the violas and the cellos. Together they make up the string section.

The brass instruments are in front of the percussion section. French horns, trumpets, trombones, and tubas make up this section. The trumpets can usually be heard over the rest of the orchestra.

The woodwind instruments are directly in front of the conductor. This section includes the flutes and piccolos, oboes and English horns, clarinets, bassoons, and saxophones.

1. Who or what is talked about most?

_____

2. Classify these details from the above passage.
   kettledrums, other drums, and just about anything else that makes a sound when it's hit or shaken
   violins, violas, and the cellos
   French horns, trumpets, trombones, and tubas
   flutes and piccolos, oboes and English horns, clarinets, bassoons, and saxophones

   These are all instruments that:

_____

Part C - Main Idea

Now that you have decided who or what is talked about most in the Part B passage, and you have classified the details, you are ready to make a main idea statement. By filling in the boxes below with the information you figured out in Part B, you will have a good main idea statement.

First: Identify who or what is talked about the most.	Next: Classify what is being said about the person or thing.

That is your main idea statement. "Sections of an orchestra are made up of many different instruments."
A good main idea statement

1. Tells who or what is talked about most
2. Classifies the details in the passage

NOTE: A detail from a passage is never a main idea statement.

Part D - Literal Questions

Directions: Read the paragraph below. Then answer the literal questions. NOTE: There are TWO correct answers to each question.

Across the Potomac River from the nation's capital, simple white marble headstones stretch in perfect, endless rows across 420 sacred acres. Arlington National Cemetery, in Arlington, Virginia, is the final resting place of 175,000 American soldiers and military leaders.

The cemetery was once an estate that belonged to George Washington Parke Curtis, the grandson of Martha Washington. Later, it belonged to Robert E. Lee, commander of the Confederate armies. Union troops took over the estate during the Civil War. In 1864 it was declared a national cemetery when the first Civil War burials occurred. The Curtis-Lee mansion, still standing on a hill that overlooks the cemetery, is known today as Arlington House, the Robert E. Lee Memorial.

In addition to miles of individual graves, monuments honor groups of dead soldiers. After the Civil War, the remains of more than 2,000 unidentified soldiers who died in the battles around Bull Run, Virginia, were moved to Arlington. The Tomb of the Unknowns is located in Arlington National Cemetery. The tomb contains the remains of an unidentified soldier from each of the four major wars in which America fought: World War I, World War II, Korea, and Vietnam. Set on a knoll, the white marble shrine is guarded by sentries day and night.

Mark the TWO correct answers to each question.

1. Which people once owned the estate that is now Arlington National Cemetery?
    a. the grandson of Martha Washington
    b. Martha Washington
    c. Robert E. Lee
    d. Abraham Lincoln

2.   The Tomb of the Unknowns contain the unidentified remains of soldiers from which wars?

    a.   Persian Gulf

    b.   Vietnam War

    c.   Civil War

    d.   World War II

3.   According to the passage, who is buried in Arlington National Cemetery?

    a.   military leaders

    b.   past presidents who have died

    c.   American soldiers

    d.   George Washington Parke Curtis

Part E - Inference

Directions: You are going to figure out how to answer a different type of inference question. Read the passage below. Think about the setting of the passage--where the action takes place--and then write a short explanation of why you think that is the setting.

I am a member of the Iroquois nation. We depend on natural resources for our basic needs. All of our food, shelter, clothing, weapons, and tools come from the forests around us. We live in villages near lakes or streams. My people live in wigwams and longhouses. Wigwams are made by bending young trees to form the round shape of the home. Pieces of tree bark are overlapped on top of this shape as protection from bad weather. Dried grass is then layered over the bark. Longhouses are rectangular in shape. They too are built of saplings and covered with bark sewn together. Sleeping platforms covered with deerskin line each wall. There are also shelves that we use for storing animal pelts, baskets, and pots.

Our clothing is made from the skins of animals, mainly deer. Skirts are made by weaving wild grasses, then covering them with animal skins.

We find food by hunting, fishing, and gathering berries, fruits, and nuts. By clearing the land, we are able to plant corn, beans, and squash. We shared this food with the white man so they could survive their first winter in a land that was new to them. We gave them seeds and showed them how to grow this food for themselves.

My people also hunt deer and small animals. A canoe, made from a hollowed out tree, along with nets and traps, are used to catch fish. During the winter months, we tap maple trees to collect the sap. After a long time cooking over a fire, the sap changes into sugar. In the winter, food is often hard for us to find. During hard times, we have had to boil our moccasins for soup, or chew on our clothing.

1. Where did this passage probably take place?

_____

2. Why do you think so?

_____

_____

Part F - Bonus

Remember, a **literal question** is answered in the passage you're reading. **Literal questions** are the easiest kind of questions to answer because you don't have to guess, or **infer,** what the answer might be; you simply have to look at what you are reading to find the answer.

Literal will be a bonus item on some quizzes or test that you take.

Literal comes from a Latin word meaning "letter."

Part G - Bonus

Inference will also be a bonus item on some quizzes or tests that you take.

Inference comes from the two Latin words *in* meaning "in," and *ferre* meaning "to carry" or "to bring." Sometimes certain things "carry in" other things with them. For example, if you see smoke, you might **infer** that there is a fire somewhere. Smoke "brings" to mind the idea of fire. Or if you see tears, you might **infer** that someone is sad because tears very often carry with them the idea that someone is sad. Nonetheless, sometimes a person cries for joy, so tears do not mean sadness. To **infer** something means that you are making a good guess. A guess can be wrong.

Optional Prosody Exercise

Part H - Reading Aloud

Directions: Listen to your teacher read the sentences below. If your teacher calls on you to read one of the sentences, try to read it so that it sounds like someone speaking. Take your time. You can read the sentence silently before reading it aloud.

1. According to the passage, who is buried in Arlington National Cemetery?

2. **Literal** comes from a Latin word meaning "letter."

3. A canoe, made from a hollowed out tree, along with nets and traps, are used to catch fish.

Lesson 8

Part A - Main Idea

Directions: After reading the passage below, follow these steps.
1. **Decide who or what is talked about the most.**
2. **Read the list of details from the passage.**
3. **Classify the details.**
4. **Use the information you gather to fill in the main idea boxes.**
5. **Write a good main idea statement.**

As a boy in Scotland in the 1850's, Alexander Graham Bell liked to experiment with sound. For example, he built a model head, with a movable tongue that could say "Mama." This interest in sound was passed on to Bell by his father and grandfather.

The cold and damp Scottish climate was partly responsible for the beginning signs of tuberculosis that Bell experienced as a young adult. He moved to Canada in 1870, and the United Sates in 1872. While in the United States, he opened a school in Boston to train teachers of deaf people. Bell also taught deaf students himself.

His interest in sound continued while he was in the US. After seeing lines of people waiting to use the telegraph, he invented a method of sending as many as eight signals over the same wire at the same time. Bell also invented a metal detector in the hope of locating bullets that were lodged in a person's body.

Bell also invented things for his own personal comfort. When it became too hot in the summer, Bell built an air cooling system...the first air conditioner!

Alexander Graham Bell's main interests continued to be sound and transmitting it over long distances. He is best known for inventing the telephone. During the invention process, he drew from previous inventions and what he knew about sound, electricity, and the human ear. His ideas all came together in 1876 when he spoke his first words into his new invention. The words were heard by his assistant in another part of the house. Bell became famous and wealthy as a result of his inventions. With the money he made, he continued to sponsor schools for the deaf and laboratories for hearing research.

1. Who or what is talked about the most?

   _____

2. Read this list of details from the passage:
    was interested in sound
    trained teachers to teach deaf people
    taught deaf students
    was responsible for many inventions
    was most famous for his invention of the telephone
    continued to sponsor schools for the deaf and laboratories for hearing research
3. Classify these details.
    These are all things someone would do or feel when:

   _____

   _____

4. Fill in the main idea boxes with the information you have gathered above.

First: Identify who or what is talked about the most.	Next: Classify what is being said about the person or thing.

NOTE: Remember, a detail from a passage is *never* a main idea statement.

5. The main idea of the passage is

_____

_____

_____

Part B - Literal Questions

Directions: Read the passage below. Then answer the literal questions. NOTE: Now there is just ONE correct answer to each question.

Under ordinary temperatures, all matter exists in one of three forms: solid, liquid, or gas. The molecules that make up matter behave differently in each form. For example, if the matter is in a solid state, the molecules are in a fixed pattern. This would be like children sitting in rows of desks in a classroom. A solid has a certain size and shape. If the matter were in a liquid state, the molecules would be able to change position and move past each other. To understand what that would be like, imagine students on the playground.

A solid also has a size or volume. Volume means it takes up space. But milk, a liquid, doesn't have a definite shape. It takes the shape of its container. Finally, if the matter were in the form of a gas, the molecules are spread apart. This would be like everyone leaving the movie theater at the end of the show. A gas is matter that has no shape or size of its own. Gases have no color either.

There is also a fourth state of matter called plasma. The molecules in plasma have been separated into particles that are electrically charged. The matter that makes up the sun and other stars is in the plasma state. Scientists are trying a process that would allow the stars to produce large amounts of electromagnetic energy. However, temperatures of millions of degrees are needed to start this process. This process is known as nuclear fusion.

Mark the correct answer to each question.

1. Under normal temperatures, matter exists in how many states?

    a. four

    b. two

    c. three

    d. five

2. The fourth state of matter is called:

    a. electromagnetic energy

    b. plasma

    c. nuclear fission

    d. hydropower

3. Where can the fourth state of matter be found?

    a. beneath the ocean floor

    b. the stars

    c. the center of the earth

    d. the upper atmosphere

4. Which form of matter could be compared to people attending a play?

    a. solid

    b. plasma

    c. gas

    d. liquid

Part C - Inference

Directions: You are going to figure out a different type of inference question. Re-read the passage in Part B. After reading the question below, think about the setting--where the action takes place--and then write a short explanation of why you think this is the setting.

1. Where do you think experiments on the fourth form of matter probably take place?

_____

2. Why do you think so?

_____

_____

Part D - Bonus

When you answer a **literal question**, you can either use some of the words that you read, or you can use other words that mean the same thing. For example, if a passage told you that an apple was the size of a ping pong ball, and you were asked a question about how big the apple in the passage was, you could say, "It is the size of a ping pong ball," or you could say, "It is tiny."

Literal will be a bonus item on some quizzes or test that you take.

Literal comes from a Latin word meaning "letter."

To learn **literal,** you will have to know what it means, how to spell it, and where it comes from.

Part E - Bonus

Remember, **inference** means "guessing about something from another thing that you already know." You **inferred** the setting in this lesson even though the passage doesn't directly tell you where the action took place.

Inference comes from Latin

Inference will be a bonus item on some quizzes or tests that you take.

To learn **inference,** you will have to know what it means, how to spell it, and where it comes from.

Optional Prosody Exercise

Part F - Reading Aloud

Directions: Listen to your teacher read the sentences below. If your teacher calls on you to read one of the sentences, try to read it so that it sounds like someone speaking. Take your time. You can read the sentence silently before reading it aloud.

1. But milk, a liquid, doesn't have a definite shape.

2. Where can the fourth state of matter be found?

3. For example, if the matter is in a solid state, the molecules are in a fixed pattern.

Lesson 9

Part A - Main Idea

Directions: After reading the passage below, follow these steps.
1. **Decide who or what is talked about the most.**
2. **Read the list of details from the passage.**
3. **Classify the details.**
4. **Use the information you gather to fill in the main idea boxes.**
5. **Write a good main idea statement.**

Keeping food from spoiling over long periods of time has been a problem that every generation has faced. Over the years, new methods have continually been developed to preserve food.

Read the following recipe from an 1819 cookbook describing how to keep peas from the summer until Christmas:

Shell the peas. Put them in a colander and drain excess water. Lay a cloth doubled four or five times on a table so the excess water can be absorbed and the peas can dry. Spread out the peas so the water inside the peas can evaporate. Clean, sterilize, and dry bottles. Fill them with the peas and cover with mutton suet fat to fill in the spaces between and above the peas. This will keep out the air and moisture. Cork them and set in a dry, cool place.

Another way of preserving food for short periods of time arrived in the early nineteenth century in the form of an icebox. You would have a hard time knowing it was related to the appliance you have in your kitchen today. An icebox did not make ice, it held it. The icebox had to be insulated to keep out the heat and keep in the cold. The ice was placed in the top of the icebox. As warm air rose, it came in contact with the ice and was cooled.

Large blocks of ice were chopped from frozen lakes and rivers in the winter. They were stored in ice houses where they were packed in sawdust. This kept the ice frozen from February through August.

Lesson 9

1. Who or what is talked about the most?

_____

2. Read this list of details from the passage:

   absorb water from peas
   let dry completely
   pack into clean, sterilized bottles
   keep out air and moisture with fat and by corking
   store in cool, dry place
   cut and store blocks of ice in sawdust
   place block of ice into icebox and replace as needed

3. Classify these details.

   These are all details showing that:

   _____

   _____

4. Fill in the main idea boxes with the information you have gathered above.

First: Identify who or what is talked about the most.	Next: Classify what is being said about the person or thing.

NOTE: Remember, a detail from a passage is *never* a main idea statement.

5. The main idea of the passage is

   _____

   _____

   _____

Part B - Main Idea

Directions: Below there are three sentences that refer to the passage in Part A. Two of the sentences are details about the passage. Remember, a detail from a passage is never a main idea statement.

One sentence below is the main idea of the passage. Mark the details by putting an *X* next to them. Next to the main idea write the letters *MI*.

a. _____ Mutton suet fat was necessary to keep out air and moisture when preserving peas in bottles.

b. _____ Food preservation used to be difficult.

c. _____ Blocks of ice were packed in sawdust to keep them from melting.

Part C - Literal Questions

Directions: Read the flyer below. Then answer the literal questions.

NOTE: Now there is just ONE correct answer to each question.

Mark the correct answer to each question.

10K FUN RUN

Proceeds Will Benefit the YWCA and YMCA Programs

Date: July 12

Time: 10:00 a.m.

Pre-register by: July 1

Entry Fees:
- Pre-registration: $10.00
- Day of the Race: $15.00
- Under 10 years & 60+ years: $5.00

Race will begin at Collins Park downtown. Course will proceed through Riverside Run and finish back at Collins Park.

For more information or to register call: 987-555-1234

PRIZES

First Prize
Second Prize
Third Prize
T-shirts for all participants!

Sponsored by: Marshall Sports And Trophy Shop

Mail form and entry fee to:

George Marshall
3725 Covey Lane
Homestead, OK 98765

Sex _____ Age on race day _____

T-shirt size: S   M   L   XL

_____
Signature   Date

Name
_____

Address
_____

_____

Phone
_____

_____
Signature of parent or guardian   Date
If under 18 years of age.

1. According to the flyer, each participant will receive:

    a.   a key chain

    b.   a t-shirt

    c.   a gift certificate from the sports shop

    d.   a small trophy

2. The race is sponsored by:

    a.   the YMCA

    b.   George Marshall

    c.   Marshall Sports and Trophy Shop

    d.   the downtown merchants

3. Anyone under the age of 18 wishing to participate in the run must have:

    a.   a recent physical

    b.   a parent participating in the run also

    c.   twenty dollars for the entry fee

    d.   a parent or guardian signature

4. What is the distance of the run?

    a.   15K

    b.   10M

    c.   4K

    d.   10K

Part D - Inference

Directions: The flyer in Part C doesn't tell the answer to the following question. After re-reading the flyer, choose the answer you think is best, and then write an explanation for your choice.

1. This is an inference question: What is the most generous reason for someone to take part in this Fun Run?

    a.   try to win a prize

    b.   get their exercise for the day

    c.   to get a free t-shirt

    d.   helping raise money for a worthy cause

2. Explain your choice.

_____

_____

Part E - Fact and Opinion

When you read--and even when you just think--it is a good idea to know when what you're reading is **fact**, and when it's **opinion**.

A **fact** is something you can prove.

> **Fact**: The amount of snowfall this year is the lowest since 1998.

You can prove that this statement is true or false by checking the snowfall records dating back to 1998.

An **opinion** is something that can not be proven.

> **Opinion**: The Mustangs never should have won the tournament.

You can't prove that the team shouldn't have won. Maybe *you* think their talent wasn't as good as the other team, but maybe *someone else* thinks they had the talent and put it to good use.

Part F - Fact and Opinion

Directions: Read each statement below. Circle the letter *O* if the statement is an opinion. Circle the letter *F* if the statement is a fact.

On the line below the statement, write a sentence explaining how you made that decision.

1. If the coach of the team doesn't play every player on the team for the same amount of time, he should resign. O / F

_____

_____

2. It can be very depressing living in the Northwest during the winter because it rains so much. O / F

_____

_____

3. Shopping for fresh produce costs less at the Farmer's Market than at Tim's Market. O / F

_____

_____

4. By going to the movies during the matinee, we can save money on the tickets. O / F

_____

_____

5. The word "cool" can be used as slang word. O / F

_____

_____

6. Orange juice made from frozen concentrate tastes the same as fresh squeezed orange juice. O / F

_____

_____

Part G - Bonus

A **Literal question** is answered in the passage you're reading. The answer does not have to use the exact words used in the passage in order for it to be correct.

Literal comes from a Latin word meaning "letter."

Inference means "guessing about something from another thing that you already know." You can **infer** feelings or setting even though the passage doesn't directly tell you.

Inference comes from Latin.

Optional Prosody Exercise

Part H - Reading Aloud

Directions: Listen to your teacher read the sentences below. If your teacher calls on you to read one of the sentences, try to read it so that it sounds like someone speaking.

1. **Inference** means "guessing about something from another thing that you already know."

2. Maybe *you* think their talent wasn't as good as the other team, but maybe *someone else* thinks they had the talent and put it to good use.

3. **Literal** comes from a Latin word meaning "letter."

Lesson 10

Optional Prosody Exercise

Directions: Listen to your teacher read the sentences below. If your teacher calls on you to read one of the sentences, try to read it so that it sounds like someone speaking.

1. After you read the paragraph below, fill in the boxes.

2. Finally, write the letters MI next to the sentence that is the main idea.

3. What is the definition of "inference?"

Lesson 11

Part A - Text Organization

Directions: Read the paragraph below from the passage in Lesson 1. Pay special attention to the underlined words and phrases.

Because of these concerns, people have been motivated to search for <u>new energy sources</u>. For example, thousands of <u>windmills</u> provide the city of San Francisco, California with some of its electrical power. Located in California's Mojave Dessert is the world's largest <u>solar energy plant</u>. This plant furnishes some of the electricity needed by the city of Los Angeles, California. Mirrors focus the sunlight on tubes of mineral oil. The oil gets hot enough to boil water. The steam that is produced powers the generators.

When you think about how a passage is *organized*, it helps you understand what you're reading. Look at the *organizational map* of this passage:

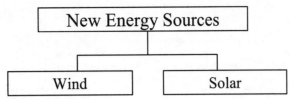

The map shows how the passage is organized. We could even plug portions of the passage into the map.

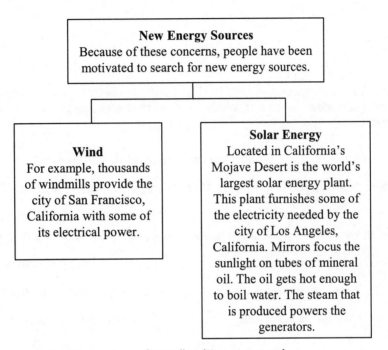

Maps such as these show clearly the structure of a well-written paragraph.

Part B - Text Organization

Directions: Read the short paragraph below, and then follow the instructions.

Martella's family has two pets, a dog and a cat. The dog is great. She's huge, but no one has any reason to be afraid of her. That dog is ready to play with anyone, at any time. Martella's cat, though, is downright mean. He hisses at anyone who gets close to him. Sometimes, he doesn't wait for you to get close. He charges you, out of the blue, for no apparent reason. That cat scares me to death.

1. Circle the text in the passage that talks about the dog.
2. Fill in the empty box below.

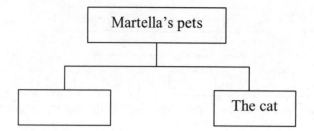

Part C - Main Idea

Directions: Put an X next to the *three* statements that just tell details from the passage. Write *MI* next to the statement that is a good main idea statement. Write *TG* next to the statement that is too general to be a good main idea statement.

A kaleidoscope is a toy through which you can see brightly colored patterns. The name of this invention is taken from three Greek words that mean "view beautiful forms."

The kaleidoscope was actually invented to interest young people in science, particularly in the science of reflection. If you look through the eyepiece, you will see a symmetrical pattern with many colored objects repeated several times. In a symmetrical pattern, opposite sides are exactly the same. The arrangement looks something like a snowflake that has been magnified and colored in.

At the end opposite the eyepiece is something called an object box. The object box is made from two pieces of plexiglass. The inside one is clear and the outside one is frosted. In between those two pieces of plexiglass are many brightly colored beads or small pieces of transparent plexiglass.

In the middle of the kaleidoscope are two mirrors that are hinged together. Each mirror reflects the pattern from one to the other. The angle at which the mirrors are attached will determine the number of images you see.

Someone once figured out how unique the images a kaleidoscope makes are. Say for example, you had a kaleidoscope that contained twenty colored beads and you changed the pattern ten times a minute by shaking it. It would take 462,880,899,576 years and 360 days to work through all the possible changes. Pretty wild, huh?

a. _____ In Greek, the word kaleidoscope means "view beautiful forms."

b. _____ The kaleidoscope was invented to interest children in science.

c. _____ The colored beads, glass, and mirrors found in kaleidoscopes are an example of the scientific concept of reflection.

d. _____ Some toys help teach science.

e. _____ The angle of the hinged mirrors in the middle of a kaleidoscope determine the number different images you'll see.

Part D - Literal

Directions: Read the thank you note below. Then answer the literal questions.

Dear Mrs. Anderson,

Thank you very much for coming to our classroom to help us with our unit on Greece. We thought the coolest things you showed us were the videos you took while you were visiting Greece last summer.

On March 15, at the end of the unit, each team is going to prepare some Greek food and bring in enough for everyone to sample. Maybe you can come back for that too!

Sincerely,

Mrs. Peterson's Class

Jenny, Alex
Joey, Steven
Emily
Patrick
Gretchen
Kate, Joe
Casey, Peter
Brad, Lie
Connie
Kristen
Steven J.
Marty
TJ, Michael
Liz, Melissa

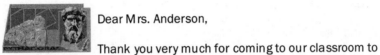

Thank You

1. The students are working on a unit about the country of:

   a. Rome

   b. Greece

   c. Italy

   d. Switzerland

2. According to the thank you note, what did Mrs. Anderson share with the class when she visited?

    a. recipes for some of the food she ate while on vacation

    b. souvenirs she bought for gifts

    c. videos taken while on her trip

    d. a photo album of her trip

3. The class would like her to come back:

    a. to help prepare the food

    b. at the end of the unit

    c. when they study their next unit

    d. on the last day of school

4. The food to be shared at the end of the unit will be prepared by:

    a. a local restaurant

    b. the school cafeteria

    c. Mrs. Anderson and Mrs. Peterson

    d. groups of students in the class

Part E - Inference

Directions: The passage doesn't tell the answer to the following question about the setting: Where does the action take place? After reading the passage, choose the answer you think is best, and then write an explanation for your choice.

In Cleveland, Ohio, there is an interesting tourist attraction to visit. It opened in September 1995, and is filled with exhibits that feature famous performers such as the Beatles and Michael Jackson. There is a jukebox with 25,000 songs to choose from, including songs by Elvis Presley. A. J. Hammer once hosted a presentation called "Rock Across America" there. There is also an educational office that publishes a magazine four times a year for teachers to use in their classrooms. It even published an article called "Teachers Make Good Rockers." For those who are interested, there are courses offered in the summer.

1. The setting for the tourist attraction in this passage is probably:

    a. a music store

    b. a music camp

    c. a rock and roll museum

    d. a concert hall where musical groups perform

2. Explain your choice.

_____

_____

Part F - Bonus

There are many types of stories. One type is called a **fable**. You might have heard of Aesop's Fables, a famous collection of many **fables**, including one of the most famous **fables** ever, the story of the "Tortoise and the Hare."

Fables are obviously fiction. The characters are usually animals, or plants, or even objects such as rocks. These characters talk, and think, and generally act like people.

A **fable** often has "a point" or "a moral" to the story. For example, the hare loses the race with the tortoise because the hare got too overconfident and cocky, while the tortoise was patient.

Fable comes from Latin and means "speak" or "a tale."

To learn **fable**, you will have to know what it means, how to spell it, and where it comes from.

Part G - Reading Aloud

Directions: Listen to your teacher read the sentences below. If your teacher calls on you to read one of the sentences, try to read it so that it sounds like someone speaking.

1. These characters talk, and think, and generally act like people.

2. According to the thank you note, what did Mrs. Anderson share with the class when she visited?

3. In Cleveland, Ohio, there is an interesting tourist attraction to visit.

Lesson 12

Part A - Text Organization

Directions: Read the paragraph below from the passage in Lesson 2, and then follow the instructions.

Television ratings try to estimate how many people are watching various television programs. Television programs with high ratings can charge advertisers more money to run commercials than less popular shows can. Because most television stations rely on advertising to pay for their costs, low-rated programs usually get cancelled

1. Circle the text in the passage that talks about low ratings.
2. Fill in the empty box below.

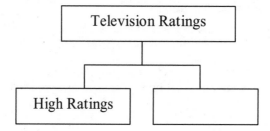

Part B - Main Idea

Directions: Put an X next to the three statements that just tell details from the passage. Write MA next to the statement that tells what the passage is mostly about.

Everyone has experienced the unusually deep breath called a yawn. It happens when you are sleepy, bored, or when you see someone else yawning. Yawning is an involuntary reflex. An involuntary reflex means you have no control over the action. Another example of an involuntary reflex is blinking your eyes if something gets too close to your face. You don't have to think about it, it happens automatically. So, once a yawn has started, it is almost impossible to stop. You can try to keep your mouth closed, but the yawning muscles still contract.

Scientists are not sure what part of the nervous system controls yawning, but it may be controlled by the section of the brain called the "midbrain." When an individual is quiet and her muscles are relaxed, breathing may become shallow. During that time of shallow breathing, the amount of air she takes in drops. If the shallow breathing continues for too long, not enough oxygen reaches the alveoli. The alveoli are millions of tiny sacs that store air in the lungs. Without enough oxygen, a yawn is most likely to occur. The deep breath that comes through a wide open mouth during a yawn brings fresh air down into the lungs, and oxygen to all of the alveoli. It also stretches the muscles and helps the blood to circulate.

Put an X next to the three statements that just tell details from the passage. Write MA next to the statement that tells what the passage is mostly about.

a. _____ The alveoli are tiny sacs in the lungs that store oxygen.

b. _____ Yawning will help get the blood circulating through the body.

c. _____ A yawn can result from periods of shallow breathing.

d. _____ A yawn is an involuntary reflex during which the body replenishes oxygen in the lungs.

Part C - Literal

Directions: Re-read the passage about kaleidoscopes from Part C of Lesson 11. Then, answer the following questions.

1. The kaleidoscope was invented in order to:

   a. produce a new toy for the market

   b. interest children in science

   c. recycle glass and old beads

   d. provide an extra credit math problem

2. Which part of the kaleidoscope determines how many images a person can see?

   a. the object box

   b. the hinged mirrors

   c. the eyepiece

   d. the frosted piece of plexiglass

3. The Greek word kaleidoscope means:

    a. "brightly colored snowflakes"

    b. "the changing world of color"

    c. "view beautiful forms"

    d. "colored reflections"

4. According to the article, what does it mean if a pattern is symmetrical?

    a. opposite sides are the same

    b. no two sides are the same

    c. the pattern is repeated over and over again

    d. the pattern keeps changing

Part D - Inference

Directions: The passage about kaleidoscopes doesn't tell the answer to the following question. After re-reading the passage, think about the feelings someone might experience when looking through one. Then, choose the answer you think is best, and write an explanation for your choice.

1. This is an inference question: How would a child probably feel while playing with a kaleidoscope?

    a. frightened

    b. bored

    c. angry

    d. entertained

2. Explain your choice.

_____

_____

Part E - Bonus

Fable will be a bonus item on some quizzes or tests that you take. In **fables**, the characters are usually animals, plants, or even objects such as rocks. These characters talk, and think, and generally act like people.

Fable comes from Latin and means "speak" or a "tale."

To learn **fable**, you will have to know what it means, how to spell it, and where it comes from.

BONUS REVIEW

Remember, **anaphora** is pronounced like this:

uh•NA•for•uh

Anaphora means "a pronoun or other words used to refer to some other word or name."

Anaphora comes from the Greek language. *Ana* means "up" and *pherein* means "carry" in Greek.

Anaphora will be a bonus item on some quizzes or tests that you take.

Optional Prosody Exercise

Part F- Reading Aloud

Directions: Listen to your teacher read the sentences below. If your teacher calls on you to read one of the sentences, try to read it so that it sounds like someone speaking.

1. **Fable** comes from Latin and means "speak" or a "tale."

2. Which part of the kaleidoscope determines how many images a person can see?

3. You don't have to think about it, it happens automatically.

Lesson 13

Part A - Text Organization

Directions: Read the short paragraph below, and then follow the instructions.

Catalina had three chores to do on Saturday morning. She had to make her bed first. She didn't like to make her bed because she had to pull it away from the wall first. Next, she had to feed the dog. She liked that job because the dog always acted so happy at feeding time. Finally, she thoroughly dusted and vacuumed her little brother's room. She liked doing that because her brother had allergies, and the dusting helped him feel better.

1. Circle the text in the passage that talks about the second thing that Catalina did.
2. Fill in the empty box below to show what Catalina did after she made her bed, but before she dusted.

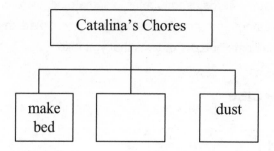

Part B - Main Idea

Directions: Put an *X* next to the three statements that just tell details from the passage. Write *MI* next to the statement that tells the main idea of the passage.

Wouldn't you love to pack your bags and fly off to Australia to go SCUBA diving off the Great Barrier Reef? Wouldn't you be thrilled if you could take a cruise around the world to see the Pyramids in Egypt? These would truly be epic adventures. But what really is an epic?

An epic is actually defined as a specific kind of poetry, and one of the major forms of literature. An epic retells the life and works of a heroic or mythological person or group of people.

Epics originated in ancient Greece and strictly speaking, in order for a work of literature to be considered an epic, it must contain many elements. An epic must:

-be very long;

-be about a serious or traditional subject;

-be written in a formal and dignified tone;

-contain many figures of speech;

-focus on the journey of a hero who represents the values of a group of people and that group's fate will depend on the outcome of the hero's journey;

-have most of its action take place across a broad geographic area;

-contain superhuman feats of strength;

-begin with the narrator calling to a muse to inspire him or her;

-begin in the middle of the action;

-discuss many heroes and important characters and must not focus on commoners or peasants.

The classic example of an epic is The Odyssey by Homer. The original Greek text of The Odyssey was 12,110 lines long. Can you imagine writing a poem that is 12,110 lines long?

Writing epic poetry, or long poems in general, has become rare in modern times. The term "epic" however has been come to be used to refer to prose works and movies which are very long, have multiple settings, large numbers of characters, or take place over a long time.

Put an X next to the three statements that just tell details from the passage. Write MI next to the statement that tells the main idea of the passage.

a. _____ An epic is defined as a specific kind of poetry, and one of the major forms of literature.

b. _____ Epics originated in ancient Greece.

c. _____ The original Greek text of the Odyssey was 12,110 lines long.

d. _____ An epic is a major form of literature that must contain several specific elements such as great length and superhuman heroes.

Part C - Literal

Directions: Read the flyer below. Then, answer the literal questions.

Business Hours

Monday	8:00 a.m.	to	5:00 p.m.
Tuesday	8:00 a.m.	to	5:00 p.m.
Wednesday	8:00 a.m.	to	5:00 p.m.
Thursday	8:00 a.m.	to	5:00 p.m.
Friday	11:00 a.m.	to	9:00 p.m.
Saturday	10:00 a.m.	to	2:00 p.m.
Sunday	Closed	to	Closed

Appointments must be cancelled within 24 hours or you will be charged for the appointment.

1. On which day of the week would you **not** be able to make an appointment with this business?

    a. Monday

    b. Sunday

    c. Saturday

    d. Wednesday

2. If you don't cancel your appointment within 24 hours you:

    a. can come the following week at the same day and time

    b. may show up at any time and they'll try to work you in whenever possible

    c. will be charged for the appointment

    d. will be charged a fee of ten dollars

3. If you are a late sleeper, which two days would be best for your appointment?

    a. Saturday or Sunday

    b. Thursday or Friday

    c. Monday or Thursday

    d. Friday or Saturday

Part D - Inference

Directions: Refer to the flyer in Part C. This time you are going to answer some inference questions.

1. This flyer could apply to all of the following situations **except**:

    a. seeing the dentist to get a cavity filled

    b. buying groceries

    c. going to the doctor's office for a check-up

    d. getting a haircut

2. Because of the hours posted, which statement probably best describes the owner of this business?

    a. The owner of the business is lazy and allows days during the week when it's possible to sleep in late.

    b. This business person understands that some people are unable to come in during the week between 8:00 a.m. and 5:00 p.m. because of school or work hours.

    c. These business hours show the owner is greedy by trying to stay open as many hours as possible.

    d. The owner is fearful of losing customers if the business doesn't stay open late and on the weekends.

Part E - Bonus

One of the most famous **fables** ever is the story of the "Tortoise and the Hare." A **fable** often has "a point" or "a moral" to the story. For example, the hare loses the race with the tortoise because the hare got too overconfident and cocky, while the tortoise was patient.

Fable comes from Latin and means "speak" or "a tale."

To learn **fable**, you will have to know what it means, how to spell it, and where it comes from.

BONUS REVIEW

Remember, **inference** is pronounced like this:

   IN•fur•unse

Inference means "guessing about something from another thing that you already know."

To learn **inference**, you will have to know what it means, how to spell it, and where it comes from.

Optional Prosody Exercise

Part F- Reading Aloud

Directions: Your teacher is *not* going to read the sentences below. If your teacher calls on you to read one of the sentences, try to read it so that it sounds like someone speaking.

1.   The owner of the business is lazy and allows days during the week when it's possible to sleep in late.

2.   If you are a late sleeper, which two days would be best for your appointment?

3.   Writing epic poetry, or long poems in general, has become rare in modern times.

Lesson 14

Part A - Text Organization

Directions: Read the paragraph from the passage in Lesson 2, and then follow the instructions.

Tim and his friends, Joe and Kate, saw the posters and decided to launch "Operation Find Buster." First, they told their parents what they had in mind, and got their permission. Then, they packed some water, some snacks, and some doggie treats in case they found Buster. The group got on their bikes and began to search the neighborhood for Buster. Early in the afternoon, they found

Buster walking along the railroad tracks at the edge of town. They returned him to his family. The family was overjoyed to see Buster, who was hungry, but safe and sound. Tim and his friends had agreed ahead of time they wouldn't accept the reward money, even though they were all saving for something special.

1. Circle the text in the passage that talks about Tim and his friends actually finding Buster.
2. Fill in the empty box below to show what happened while searching for Buster.

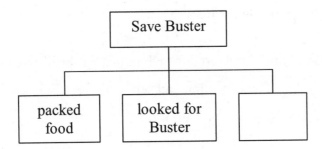

Part B - Main Idea

Directions: Re-read the passage below from Lesson 11. Place an *X* beside the three phrases that just tell details from the passage and then place *GT* beside the phrase that would be a good title for the passage.

In Cleveland, Ohio, there is an interesting tourist attraction to visit. It opened in September 1995, and is filled with exhibits that feature famous performers such as the Beatles and Michael Jackson. There is a jukebox with 25,000 songs to choose from, including songs by Elvis Presley. A. J. Hammer once hosted a presentation called "Rock Across America" there. There is also an educational office that publishes a magazine four times a year for teachers to use in their classrooms. It even published an article called "Teachers Make Good Rockers." For those who are interested, there are courses offered in the summer.

a. _____ *Turn Down That Music!*

b. _____ *Famous Performers Visit Cleveland, Ohio*

c. _____ *Rocking and Rolling in Cleveland, Ohio*

d. _____ *Teachers Make Good Rockers*

Part C - Literal

Directions: Read the passage below. Then, answer the literal questions.

In the song "Give a Man a Fish," the popular rap group Arrested Development sings the following lyric:

Give a man a fish, and he'll eat for a day....
Teach him how to fish and he'll eat forever.

This lyric is actually a famous proverb, or saying, that has been spoken for over a hundred years. It talks about the value of an education and self-reliance. If you learn to do something for yourself, you don't have to rely on others to do it for you.

Other proverbs are famous, too. "Necessity is the mother of invention" and "build a better mousetrap" sound different but both mean similar things: we tend to invent new things only when we need to. For example, the ancient Romans needed a way to build bridges that could cross large valleys and could hold heavy weight. Roman engineers experimented with a variety of bridges before they invented the Roman Arch. Today, many structures are built using arches, because they are unusually strong, but require few materials.

Other sayings are meant to give advice. "Nothing will come out of nothing" is another way of saying, "You never know what you can do unless you try." "Strike while the iron is hot" is another way of telling someone to take advantage of an opportunity.

Proverbs serve different purposes. They give encouragement, as in, "it's never over till it's over." They can also warn people, as in, "the road to hell is paved with good intentions." Proverbs mean all sorts of things. Just remember, "There's more than one way to skin a cat!"

1. According to the passage, the best definition of a proverb is:
    a.   a phrase or lyric in a popular song
    b.   new sayings that are invented using slang words
    c.   a saying that has been spoken for over a hundred years
    d.   phrases that are annoying because they have hidden meanings

2. Many structures are built using arches because:

   a.   few materials are needed to build them and they are extremely strong

   b.   arches provide the height needed for large trucks to pass under the bridges

   c.   they provide a pleasing look to bridges and buildings that would otherwise be too plain

   d.   many construction companies don't have the money needed to build structures without using arches

3. Which proverb would you use if you were trying to encourage a friend to be patient?

   a.   "it's never over till it's over"

   b.   "nothing will come out of nothing"

   c.   "build a better mousetrap"

   d.   "there's more than one way to skin a cat!"

Part D - Inference

Directions: Read the following passage and then answer the questions.

Everything was going fine between Anna and her friends. But then, out of the blue, some of Anna's friends began sending her e-mails that were unkind. Not only that, but she began to get phone calls at home from her friends, demanding to know why Anna had been spreading rumors about them around school. Anna had no idea why this was happening to her. She had never said anything unkind about any of her friends. Of course, Anna was very upset, but she didn't know what to do. It seemed that every time she tried to deny something and stand up for herself, things just got worse. Tia, one of Anna's friends, asked the teacher for some time to talk to the whole class. She had Anna stand beside her and, in no uncertain terms, told the class that Anna had not been talking about them. She also said that the behavior of some of them was very hurtful, and it needed to stop.

When the matter was finally settled, Tia began to ask Anna if she could copy her math homework. She then started calling her on the phone and asking Anna if she could borrow some of her clothes. Anna was grateful for what Tia had done, but it seemed like she now had a whole new problem to deal with.

1. The passage doesn't tell you the answer to this question, so think carefully about what you read: which of the following proverbs would best apply to this passage?

   a. "don't look a gift horse in the mouth"

   b. "don't get your nose out of joint"

   c. "a friend in need is a friend indeed"

   d. "bite the dust"

2. Write a short explanation for your choice in the first question.

_____

_____

_____

Part E - Bonus

Fables are obviously fiction. The characters are usually animals, plants, or even objects such as rocks. These characters talk, and think, and generally act like people.

Fable comes from Latin and means "speak" or "a tale."

To learn **fable**, you will have to know what it means, how to spell it, and where it comes from.

BONUS REVIEW

Literal comes from the Latin word *littera* (LIT er ah), which means "letter" or "word."

When you take a reading test, some of the questions you have to answer are **literal** questions. That means that you can find the answer to the questions in the passage you are reading.

To learn **literal**, you will have to know what it means, how to spell it, and where it comes from.

Optional Prosody Exercise

Part F- Reading Aloud

Directions: Your teacher is *not* going to read the sentences below. If your teacher calls on you to read one of the sentences, try to read it so that it sounds like someone speaking.

1. When you take a reading test, some of the questions you have to answer are **literal** questions.

2. Which proverb would you use if you were trying to encourage a friend to be patient?

3. For example, the ancient Romans needed a way to build bridges that could cross large valleys and could hold heavy weight.

Lesson 15

Optional Prosody Exercise

Directions: Your teacher is *not* going to read the sentences below. If your teacher calls on you to read one of the sentences, try to read it so that it sounds like someone speaking.

1. If a 1st place ribbon was to be given to the toughest living thing on earth, do you know what would win?

2. The passage doesn't tell you exactly, but after reading the model sentence, which statement would best describe the word "briny?"

3. Sometimes she would stir melted chocolate chips and coconut into the dough, shape them into balls and then roll them in powered sugar.

Lesson 16

Part A- Text Organization

Directions: Read the paragraph below, and then follow the instructions.

Under ordinary temperatures, all matter exists in one of three forms: solid, liquid, or gas. The molecules that make up matter behave differently in each form. For example, if the matter is in a solid state, the molecules are in a fixed pattern. A solid has a certain size and shape. If the matter were in a liquid state, the molecules would be able to change position and move past each other. Liquids don't have a definite shape. They take on the shape of their containers. Finally, matter in the form of a gas has molecules that are spread apart. A gas is matter that has no shape or size of its own. Gases have no color either.

1. Circle the text that talks about solids.
2. Circle the text that talks about gasses.
3. Fill in the empty space.

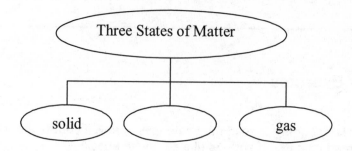

Part B - Author's Purpose

Read the passage below.

Before the industrial revolution, the job of separating cotton seeds from the cotton fibers was a slow process that had to be done by hand. After Eli Whitney's invention of the cotton gin, this process could be completed quickly. In one day, the cotton gin could clean as much cotton as 50 people could working by hand. The region benefited greatly from this invention, and cotton became one of its primary crops. Cotton growing became more profitable after the invention of the cotton gin, and the demand for slaves to work in the cotton fields increased.

Whitney and a partner manufactured the cotton gin, but a factory fire prevented them from making enough gins to meet the demand. Other manufacturers began to copy his invention. For years Whitney fought many legal battles to protect the patent on his invention. Owning the patent gave him the right to be the only one to manufacture it. He eventually won the protection of his patent, but the U.S. Congress then refused to renew it once it had expired. He profited very little from his invention.

But Eli Whitney was not done. During all those years of fighting for his patent, he developed a way to mass produce muskets for the federal government. Mass producing something means large numbers of it can be made quickly, without wasted time or materials. By using interchangeable machine-made parts in making the muskets, Whitney laid the groundwork for mass producing all kinds of goods in factories.

Directions: Use the checklist below to determine if the author's purpose is to inform, entertain, or persuade. Put a check next to the statements that are true for the passage you just read. Then, answer the questions.

Inform	Entertain	Persuade
1. The passage sounds like a textbook or an encyclopedia. ___	1. The passage sounds like a story.___	1. The passage sounds like an advertisement. ___
2. The author is trying to teach you some facts that might be new to you. ___	2. The author is not trying to teach you any facts.___	2. The author is using facts to change your mind about something.___
3. The author does not try to influence your feelings. ___	3. The author tries to make you feel some emotion, such as happiness, sadness, or fear.___	3. The author has an obvious opinion and tries to convince you to feel the same way.___

The list with the most checks will tell you the author's purpose. Which list has the most checks?

a. inform

b. entertain

c. persuade

Therefore, the author's general purpose is to:

a. inform

b. entertain

c. persuade

Part C - Main Idea

Directions: Place an X next to three details from the passage in Part B. Write *S* next to the statement that is a summary of the passage.

a. _____ Many manufacturers copied and produced the cotton gin.

b. _____ The inventor, Eli Whitney, struggled to get the credit he deserved for inventing the cotton gin, but he was recognized as a leader in mass producing items.

c. _____ As a result of the cotton gin, more slaves were needed to work in the cotton fields.

d. _____ When done by hand, separating the cotton seeds from the fiber can be slow work.

Part D- Review

Directions: Re-read the passage in Part B, and then answer the literal and inference questions

1. How did Eli Whitney probably feel when others began to manufacture his invention?

    a.   satisfied that he had done his best

    b.   confused about what to do next

    c.   proud that others wanted to copy his invention

    d.   angry and frustrated with the legal system

2. The passage doesn't tell you exactly, but the setting for the use of the cotton gin is probably in:

    a.   The North

    b.   The South

    c.   The Southwest

    d.   The Plains

3. Write a short explanation for your choice in question number two.

    _____

    _____

    _____

4. What did the cotton gin actually do?

    a.   picked the cotton balls from the stalk of the plant

    b.   cleaned the dirt and any insects from the cotton

    c.   separated the seeds from the cotton fiber

    d.   planted the cotton seeds in evenly spaced rows

5. Which words from the passage show that Eli Whitney did not become rich from the invention of the cotton gin?

    a.   ...fought many legal battles...

    b.   Cotton growing became more profitable...

    c.   ...profited very little from his invention.

    d.   ...began to copy his invention.

6. What was the first incident that prevented Whitney from manufacturing enough cotton gins?

    a. He became ill and couldn't work.

    b. A fire destroyed his factory.

    c. There weren't enough workers in the factory to handle the demand.

    d. The court system shut down his factory because he didn't have a patent on his invention.

Part E- Bonus

Starting with Lesson 11, you have been doing "text organization" activities. Here is the diagram from Part A of this lesson:

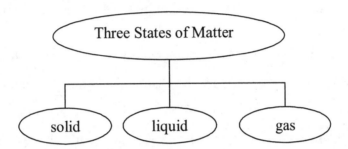

The different types of diagrams in the text organization exercises are sometimes called **cognitive maps**. Basically, the word **cognition** means "thinking." As you know, a map is a representation of something. The most familiar maps are representations of cities, states, and countries. A **cognitive map** is a representation of someone's thinking. When you read, a **cognitive map** represents the author's thinking. When you write, you can use a **cognitive map** to organize your own thinking.

The word **cognitive** comes from Greek. *Co-* is a variation of *com-*, which means "with" or "together." The base of the word is *gno*, which means "to know." When you're getting your knowledge together and organized, that's thinking, or **cognition**.

To learn **cognitive map**, you will have to know what it means, how to spell it, and where it comes from.

BONUS REVIEW

Remember, a **fable** often has "a point" or "a moral" to the story. For example, the hare loses the race with the tortoise because the hare got too overconfident and cocky, while the tortoise was patient.

Fable comes from Latin and means "speak" or a "tale."

Optional Prosody Exercise

Part F- Reading Aloud

Directions: If your teacher calls on you to read one of the sentences, try to read it so that it sounds like someone speaking.

1. Remember, a **fable** often has "a point" or "a moral" to the story.

2. Many manufacturers copied and produced the cotton gin.

Lesson 17

Part A - Text Organization

Directions: Read the paragraph below, and then follow the instructions.

Here is a recipe from an 1819 cookbook, describing how to keep peas until Christmas:

Shell the peas. Put them in a colander and drain excess water. Lay a cloth on a table, doubled over four or five times, so the excess water can be absorbed and the peas can dry. Spread out the peas so the water inside the peas can evaporate. Clean, sterilize, and dry bottles. Fill them with the peas and cover with mutton suet fat to fill in the spaces between and above the peas. This will keep out the air and moisture. Cork them and set in a dry, cool place.

1. Circle the text that talks about drying the peas.
2. Circle the text that talks about filling the bottles.
3. Fill in the empty spaces.

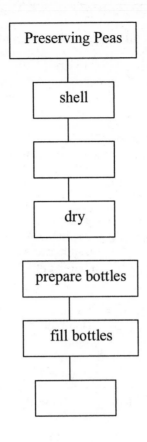

Part B - Author's Purpose

Read the passage below from Lesson 14.

Everything was going fine between Anna and her friends. But then, out of the blue, some of Anna's friends began sending her e-mails that were unkind. Not only that, but she began to get phone calls at home from her friends, demanding to know why Anna had been spreading rumors about them around school. Anna had no idea why this was happening to her. She had never said anything unkind about any of her friends.

Of course, Anna was very upset, but she didn't know what to do. It seemed that every time she tried to deny something and stand up for herself, things just got worse. Tia, one of Anna's friends, asked the teacher for some time to talk to the whole class. She had Anna stand beside her and, in no uncertain terms, told the class that Anna had not been talking about them. She also said the behavior of some of them was very hurtful and it needed to stop.

When the matter was finally settled, Tia began to ask Anna if she could copy her math homework. She then started calling her on the phone and asking Anna if she could borrow some of her clothes. Anna was grateful for what Tia had done, but it seemed like she now had a whole new problem to deal with.

Directions: Use the checklist below to determine if the author's purpose is to inform, entertain, or persuade. Put a check next to the statements that are true for the passage you just read. Then, answer the questions.

Inform	Entertain	Persuade
1. The passage sounds like a textbook or an encyclopedia.__	1. The passage sounds like a story. __	1. The passage sounds like an advertisement.__
2. The author is trying to teach you some facts that might be new to you. __	2. The author is not trying to teach you any facts.__	2. The author is using facts to change your mind about something. __
3. The author does not try to influence your feelings. __	3. The author tries to make you feel some emotion, such as happiness, sadness, or fear. __	3. The author has an obvious opinion and tries to convince you to feel the same way. __

1. The list with the most checks will tell you the author's purpose. Which list has the most checks?

    a. inform

    b. entertain

    c. persuade

2. Therefore, the author's general purpose is to:

    a. inform

    b. entertain

    c. persuade

Part C - Main Idea

Directions: Put an *X* next to the *three* statements that just tell details from the passage. Then, write *MI* next to the statement that is a good main idea statement. Finally, write TG next to the statement that is TOO GENERAL to be a good main idea statement for this passage.

a. _____ Anna received unkind e-mail messages.

b. _____ Tia defended Anna in front of the class.

c. _____ Anna had some problems with friends.

d. _____ Sometimes friends can be hurtful.

e. _____ Tia asked to copy homework and borrow clothes in return for standing up for Anna.

Part D- Review

Directions: Look at the calendar and then answer the literal and inference questions.

Monthly Chore Schedule for February

S	M	T	W	T	F	S
						1
2	3 Fred dishes	4 Patty dishes	5 Joey dishes	6 Fred dishes	7 Patty dishes	8
9	10 Kid's free night!	11 Joey set table	12 Kid's free night!	13 Joey set table	14 Kid's free night!	15
16	17 Fred dishes	18 Patty dishes	19 Fred dishes	20 Patty dishes	21 Fred dishes	22
23	24 Fred set table	25 Patty set table	26 Joey clear table	27 Fred set table	28 Patty set table	

1. Making a calendar showing each person's evening chore shows this family is probably:

   a. mean

   b. boring

   c. organized

   d. well-educated

2. The person responsible for clearing the table is:

    a. Joey

    b. Patty

    c. Fred

    d. Mom

3. Write a short explanation why this calendar is a good idea.

    _____

    _____

    _____

4. According to the calendar, what shows up the most this month?

    a. clearing the table

    b. setting the table

    c. doing the dishes

    d. Kid's free night

5. Joey has the least amount of chores, but you can't tell the reason why by the information on the calendar. The best possible reason is that he:

    a. is the youngest

    b. has more homework than Fred or Patty

    c. does a sloppy job

    d. does most of the cooking

6. How many "free kid's nights" are there?

    a. five

    b. three

    c. two

    d. six

Part E- Bonus

Here is a **cognitive map** from Lesson 12:

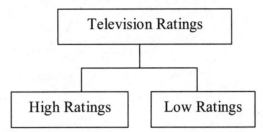

Remember that a **cognitive map** is a representation of someone's thinking. When you read, a **cognitive map** represents the author's thinking.

The word **cognitive** comes from Greek. *Co-* is a variation of *com-*, which means "with" or "together." The base of the word is *gno*, which means "to know." When you're getting your knowledge together and organized, that's thinking, or **cognition.**

To learn **cognitive map**, you will have to know what it means, how to spell it, and where it comes from.

BONUS REVIEW

Inference means "guessing about something from another thing that you already know." You figure out something that a passage doesn't tell you directly.

Part F- Reading Aloud

Directions: If your teacher calls on you to read one of the sentences, try to read it so that it sounds like someone speaking.

1. *Co-* is a variation of *com-*, which means "with" or "together."

2. But then, out of the blue, some of Anna's friends began sending her e-mails that were unkind.

Lesson 18

Part A - Text Organization

Directions: Read the paragraph below, and then follow the instructions.

Sojourner Truth was born into slavery in New York in 1795. She gained her freedom in 1827, when the state freed its slaves. After working as a servant for several years, she became a public speaker on behalf of abolition and the rights of women.

Lesson 18

1. Circle the text that talks about slavery.
2. Fill in the empty space in the diagram below.

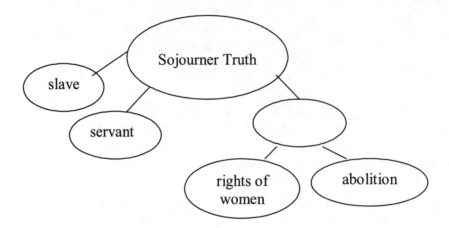

Part B - Author's Purpose

Directions: Read the passage below.

Antibiotics have been around since the year 1928 when they were discovered by Alexander Fleming. They were once known as "wonder drugs." Antibiotics have the power to fight bacterial infections, and they produce positive results quickly. If you've ever been sick and the doctor prescribed antibiotics for you, chances are you began to feel better shortly after taking them. On the down side, antibiotics do not have the ability to fight viruses.

Alexander Fleming was working in a hospital lab growing cultures of bacteria. He noticed that one of his cultures was doing very poorly. The well-rounded bacterial colonies appeared in only one part of the dish. When he looked at it closely, he noticed that a bit of mold was growing at the top part of the dish. There were no bacteria growing near the mold. He assumed that someone had left the lid off the culture dish and ruined the culture, so he threw it away.

When an assistant happened to walk by, Fleming recovered the culture dish from the trash and showed it to him. Fleming continued to study it, and curiosity got the best of him. Fleming began testing all kind of molds and he discovered the particular one that had invaded his bacteria. This is the same mold that grows on cheese, citrus fruit, and bread. At the time, the technology was not available for him to isolate the substance which we now know as penicillin from the rest of the mold. Because of this, little attention was paid to his discovery for nearly a decade.

During World War II there was a new interest in finding a natural substance that attacked bacteria. Scientists at Oxford University, in England, began to experiment with some samples of Fleming's original cultures. By now, technology was available to isolate the penicillin from the mold. Within a few years, penicillin was being used to help save the lives of men wounded in battle. In 1945, Fleming and the Oxford scientists were awarded the Nobel Prize in physiology (which is the study of living matter) and medicine.

Directions: Use the checklist below to determine if the author's purpose is to inform, entertain, or persuade. Put a check next to the statements that are true for the passage you just read. Then, answer the questions.

Inform	Entertain	Persuade
1. The passage sounds like a textbook or an encyclopedia. __	1. The passage sounds like a story. __	1. The passage sounds like an advertisement.__
2. The author is trying to teach you some facts that might be new to you. __	2. The author is not trying to teach you any facts. __	2. The author is using facts to change your mind about something. __
3. The author does not try to influence your feelings. __	3. The author tries to make you feel some emotion, such as happiness, sadness, or fear. __	3. The author has an obvious opinion and tries to convince you to feel the same way. __

1. The list with the most checks will tell you the author's purpose. Which list has the most checks?

    a. inform

    b. entertain

    c. persuade

2. Therefore, the author's general purpose is to:

    a. inform

    b. entertain

    c. persuade

Lesson 18

Part C - Main Idea

Directions: Read the paragraph below. Next, put an *X* beside the three statements that just tell details from the passage. Write *MD* next to the statement that mostly describes the passage.

The Andes is the world's longest mountain range. It runs along the western coast of South America. It is over 4,400 miles long, 300 miles wide in some parts, and the mountain range's average height is about 13,000 feet.

The mountains extend over seven countries in South America: Argentina, Bolivia, Chile, Colombia, Ecuador, Peru and Venezuela. One theory about where the name Andes comes from says it comes from the Quechua word *anti*, which means "high crest". (Quechua was the language of the Incas who were native to the Andes.) Another theory says that the name Andes comes from the Spanish word "anden" wich means terrace; this may refer to the way the Incas built terraces into the mountains so they could farm and garden.

a. _____ The Andes, home to the Incas, is the world's largest mountain range.

b. _____ The Andes runs along the western coast of South America.

c. _____ The mountain range's average height is about 13,000 feet.

d. _____ The mountains extend over seven countries in South America.

Part D- Review

Directions: Re-read the passage in Part B and then answer the literal and inference questions.

1. The passage doesn't tell you exactly, but Alexander Fleming was probably:

   a. the author of a science book

   b. a student at Oxford University

   c. a doctor

   d. a scientist

2. Briefly explain what was happening in the culture dish that contained mold.

_____

_____

_____

3. According to the passage, what are the benefits of antibiotics? (There are **two** correct answers.)

    a. Positive results are quickly seen.

    b. Antibiotics can also fight viruses.

    c. They are powerful fighters against bacteria.

    d. They can be taken in the form of a pill so you don't have to get a shot.

4. The passage doesn't tell you exactly, but which of the following is the best example of a question to which Fleming might try to find the answer?

    a. How can I keep this mold from growing in my culture dish?

    b. Who left the lid off my culture dish?

    c. Is the mold responsible for the bacteria not being able to grow?

    d. How did these guys at Oxford get samples of my cultures?

5. What kept Alexander Fleming from separating the penicillin from mold?

    a. the technology wasn't available

    b. he died before he was able to accomplish it

    c. there was no interest in his findings

    d. he was never able to find the correct type of mold

6. Fleming, along with the Oxford scientists, was awarded the:

    a. Caldecott Medal

    b. Purple Heart

    c. Nobel Prize

    d. Newbery Award

Part E - Bonus

Here is the **cognitive map** from Lesson 14.

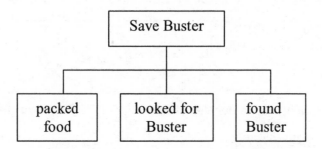

The different types of diagrams in the text organization exercises are sometimes called **cognitive maps**. Basically, the word **cognition** means "thinking." As you know, a map is a representation of something. The most familiar maps are representations of cities, states, and countries. A **cognitive map** is a representation of someone's thinking. When you write, you can use a **cognitive map** to organize your own thinking.

The word **cognitive** comes from Greek. *Co-* is a variation of *com-*, which means "with" or "together." The base of the word is *gno*, which means "to know." When you're getting your knowledge together and organized, that's thinking, or **cognition**.

To learn **cognitive map**, you will have to know what it means, how to spell it, and where it comes from.

BONUS REVIEW

Don't forget that **literal** is pronounced like this:

LIT•er•ul

Literal comes from the Latin word *littera* (LIT er ah), which means "letter" or "word."

You can find the answer to **literal** questions in the passage you are reading.

To learn **literal**, you will have to know what it means, how to spell it, and where it comes from.

Optional Prosody Exercise

Part F- Reading Aloud

Directions: If your teacher calls on you to read one of the sentences, try to read it so that it sounds like someone speaking.

1. When you write, you can use a **cognitive map** to organize your own thinking.

2. Scientists at Oxford University, in England, began to experiment with some samples of Fleming's original cultures.

Lesson 19

Part A - Text Organization

Directions: Read the paragraph below, and then follow the instructions.

Under ordinary temperatures, all matter exists in one of three forms: solid, liquid, or gas. The molecules that make up matter behave differently in each form. For example, if the matter is in a solid state, the molecules are in a fixed pattern. A solid has a certain size and shape. This would be like children sitting in rows of desks in a classroom. If the matter were in a liquid state, the molecules would be able to change position and move past each other. Liquids don't have a definite shape. They take on the shape of their containers. To understand what that would like, imagine students in a lunch room or on the playground. Finally, matter in the form of a gas has molecules are that are spread apart. This would be like everyone leaving the movie theater at the end of the show. A gas is matter that has no shape or size of its own. Gases have no color either.

1. Circle the text that gives an example of what the molecules in a solid might be like.
2. Circle the text that gives an example of what the molecules in a gas might be like.
3. Fill in the empty spaces in the diagram below.

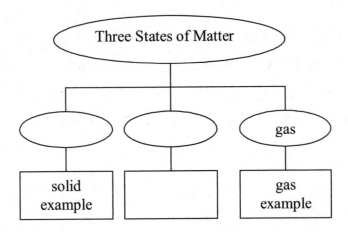

Part B - Author's Purpose

Directions: Read the passage below.

When a place experiences economic growth, many other things grow too. Population usually grows because growing businesses need to hire more people. People tend to move to communities where there are jobs. The number of houses and apartment buildings usually grows because all of the people new to the community need someplace to live. The growth of new trees, however, does not usually go along with economic growth.

New businesses and homes require space and often that means cutting down trees to make that space. Many times, whole forests are cut down to make way for new communities. And while economic growth is important, so are trees. We must find a way to allow for economic growth while not destroying one of our most precious resources.

Trees help to reduce the greenhouse effect. Heat from Earth is trapped in the atmosphere due to high levels of carbon dioxide and other gases that stop the atmosphere from releasing heat into space. This is known as the greenhouse effect. Trees remove carbon dioxide from the atmosphere during photosynthesis. They then return oxygen back to the atmosphere as a by-product. A single grown tree can take in carbon dioxide at a rate of 48 pounds per year and release enough oxygen to support two people.

Trees also reduce the greenhouse effect by shading our buildings. This reduces air conditioning needs up to 30%. Because people need less electricity to run their air conditioners, we need to burn less fuel to make electricity. Between carbon dioxide removal from the atmosphere and the cooling effect they have, trees are a very efficient tool in fighting the greenhouse effect.

We should work to make sure that when we build new buildings we plan to set aside space for parks and trees. Beautiful parks with beautiful trees are not just good for the environment, they are good for the communities where they are located. What's better than a Saturday afternoon picnic in the park under your favorite tree? Trees work every minute of every day to make our environment a healthier place for us to live. We should work to make room for them in our

communities.

Directions: Use the checklist below to determine if the author's purpose is to inform, entertain, or persuade. Put a check next to the statements that are true for the passage you just read. Then, answer the questions.

Inform	Entertain	Persuade
1. The passage sounds like a textbook or an encyclopedia.__	1. The passage sounds like a story. __	1. The passage sounds like an advertisement.__
2. The author is trying to teach you some facts that might be new to you. __	2. The author is not trying to teach you any facts. __	2. The author is using facts to change your mind about something.__
3. The author does not try to influence your feelings. __	3. The author tries to make you feel some emotion, such as happiness, sadness, or fear. __	3. The author has an obvious opinion and tries to convince you to feel the same way. __

1. The list with the most checks will tell you the author's purpose. Which list has the most checks?

    a. inform

    b. entertain

    c. persuade

2. Therefore, the author's general purpose is to:

    a. inform

    b. entertain

    c. persuade

Part C - Main Idea

Directions: Re-read the passage in Part B. Place an *X* next to the three statements that just tell details from the passage. Write *S* next to the statement that is a good summary statement

a. _____ A single grown tree can release enough oxygen to support two people.

b. _____ Trees can reduce air conditioning needs by 30%.

c. _____ We should work to protect trees because they are an important natural resource and they help keep our atmosphere healthy.

d. _____ Trees remove carbon dioxide from the atmosphere through photosynthesis.

Part D- Review

Directions: Re-read the passage below from Lesson 7 and then answer the literal and inference questions.

A modern symphony orchestra may include more than 100 musicians, playing many different musical instruments. There are four major sections in an orchestra: stringed instruments, woodwind instruments, brass instruments, and percussion instruments. Each group is seated in sections according to a traditional plan.

The percussion section is in the back. The kettledrums are the stars there. Other drums, and just about anything else that makes a sound when it's hit or shaken, may be part of the percussion section.

On the right and left of the conductor are the violins. There are usually 30 or more. Violins are the smallest of the stringed instruments. They are joined by the violas and the cellos. Together they make up the string section.

The brass instruments are in front of the percussion section. French horns, trumpets, trombones, and tubas make up this section. The trumpets can usually be heard over the rest of the orchestra.

The woodwind instruments are directly in front of the conductor. This section includes the flutes and piccolos, oboes and English horns, clarinets, bassoons, and saxophones.

1. The instruments that can be heard above all the others in an orchestra are the:

    a. violins

    b. kettle drums

    c. trumpets

    d. saxophones

2. Which of the following diagrams shows the correct placement of instruments in an orchestra?

    a.

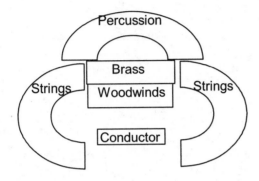

    b.

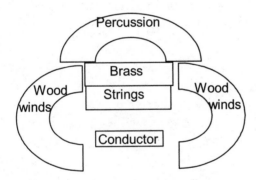

    c.

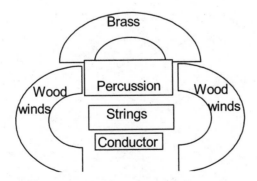

d.

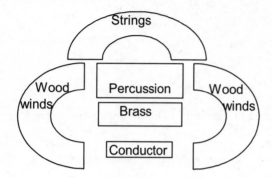

3. Which word would best describe the kettle drums in the percussion section?

    a.   peaceful

    b.   outstanding

    c.   ignored

    d.   loudest

4. Which stringed instrument is the smallest in its section?

    a.   flute

    b.   cello

    c.   violin

    d.   viola

5. According to the passage, the sections of an orchestra are based on:

    a.   the number of instruments in each section

    b.   the vote of the musicians

    c.   the wishes of the conductor

    d.   tradition

Part E- Bonus

Here is a different type of **cognitive map**, from Lesson 18.

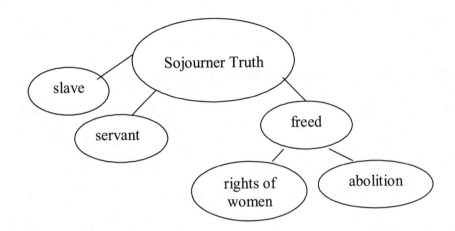

There are many varieties of **cognitive maps**. Remember, the word **cognitive** comes from Greek.

BONUS REVIEW

Remember, too that the answers to **literal** questions are found in the passage you're reading, but you have to figure out the answers to **inference** questions.

Finally, **anaphora** means "a pronoun or other words used to refer to some other word or name."

Optional Prosody Exercise

Part F- Reading Aloud

Directions: If your teacher calls on you to read one of the sentences, try to read it so that it sounds like someone speaking.

1. There are four major sections in an orchestra: stringed instruments, woodwind instruments, brass instruments, and percussion instruments.

2. Because people need less electricity to run their air conditioners, we need to burn less fuel to make electricity.

Lesson 21

Part A - Text Organization

Directions: Read the paragraph below, and then follow the instructions.

An important incident occurred in the colonial city of Boston on March 5, 1770. It started with a few colonists tormenting a British soldier who was standing guard at the Customs House. The Boston colonists didn't like having British soldiers in their city. The lone soldier threatened the colonists, who in turn called more colonists to the scene. With that increased threat, the British soldier called for more help. A small group of soldiers under the leadership of Captain Thomas Preston came to the aid of the lone soldier. The colonists, in response, surrounded Captain Preston and his men. No one knows exactly what happened next, but a soldier fired his musket into the threatening crowd. Five colonists ended up dead and several other people were hurt. No matter how it started, the incident was tragic. Sam Adams, a cousin of the future President of the United States, John Adams, took advantage of the incident as a way to help rile up more colonists to support independence from the British. Adams gave the incident a name, which inspired many colonial patriots and remains famous to this day: The Boston Massacre.

1. Circle the text that belongs in the box titled, "The Incident Itself" in the diagram below.
2. What is a good, specific title for the first box in the diagram?

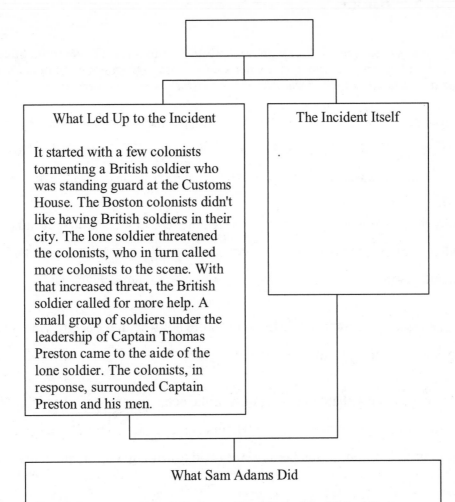

What Led Up to the Incident

It started with a few colonists tormenting a British soldier who was standing guard at the Customs House. The Boston colonists didn't like having British soldiers in their city. The lone soldier threatened the colonists, who in turn called more colonists to the scene. With that increased threat, the British soldier called for more help. A small group of soldiers under the leadership of Captain Thomas Preston came to the aide of the lone soldier. The colonists, in response, surrounded Captain Preston and his men.

The Incident Itself

What Sam Adams Did

Sam Adams, a cousin of the future President of the United States, John Adams, took advantage of the incident as a way to help rile up more colonists to support independence from the British. Adams gave the incident a name, which inspired many colonial patriots and remains famous to this day: The Boston Massacre.

Part B - Author's Purpose

To inform, to entertain, or to persuade are examples of an author's general purpose for writing. Not only is it a good idea to be able to identify an author's general purpose, but it is also good if you can state an author's specific purpose in a complete sentence.

Let's say you've read an article about how cells divide and multiply. The following would be a good **specific** statement of the author's **main purpose**:

The author's main purpose is to explain how cells divide and multiply.

Notice that a specific main purpose is just about the same thing as a main idea. So you can use the same skills you learned for figuring out the main idea when you are figuring out an author's specific purpose.

Lesson 21

Part C - Author's Purpose

Directions: In the passage below, the author's *general* purpose is to inform the reader about life during the industrial age. After reading the passage, choose a statement of the author's main *specific* purpose. Remember, the main idea is part of the statement of the author's *specific* purpose.

The industrial era affected the lives of the American people sharply. Before 1900, 25 per cent of the American people lived in cities. By the year 1916, that number had increased to 50 per cent. The population of the cities was a mix of the wealthy, the middle class, and the disadvantaged.

The wealthy business owners and investors were able to accumulate huge fortunes. The number of millionaires in the United States grew from about 20 in 1850 to more than 3,000 in 1900. These wealthy Americans were able to buy almost anything they desired.

The middle classes lived comfortable lives, but were not wealthy. The growing middle class owned small business, or were factory or office managers.

The disadvantaged didn't share in the benefits of the economic growth. The laborers who toiled in the factories, mills, and mines put in 60 hours per week for about 20 cents an hour. Many children received little or no education because they had to work to contribute to their families' income.

1. Which of the following sentences expresses the author's *specific* purpose?

    a. The author's purpose is to inform the reader about the lifestyles of the wealthy after 1900.

    b. The author's purpose is to inform readers about the occupations of the middle class living in the cities.

    c. The author's purpose is to inform the reader about the dramatic differences in city lifestyles during the age of industry.

    d. The author's purpose is to persuade the reader to move from the farm to the city for a better lifestyle

Part D- Main Idea

Directions: Re-read the passage in Part C. Put an *X* next to the *three* statements that just tell details from the passage. Write *MI* next to the statement that is a good main idea statement. Finally, write TG next to the statement that is too general to be a good main idea statement for this passage.

a. _____ Many people moved from the farms to the cities for jobs.

b. _____ Lifestyles in the city can vary greatly.

c. _____ In some families, the children were needed to work and could not attend school.

d. _____ There were dramatic differences in city lifestyles, ranging from the very wealthy to the very poor, as well as a growing middle class.

e. _____ Small business owners were not wealthy but lived comfortably.

Part E - Word Meaning

Directions: After you read each model, choose the best possible meaning for the underlined word.

1. **Model**: The laborers who <u>toiled</u> in the factories, mills, and mines put in 60 hours per week for about 20 cents an hour.

    a. owned

    b. worked

2. **Model**: The wealthy population in the city lived an <u>exorbitant</u> lifestyle, while others lived in poverty.

    a. going beyond what is considered normal

    b. comfortable and quiet

Part F - Review

Directions: Read the passage below and then answer the questions.

We live in a world that requires A LOT of energy. We need energy to make our cars run, to heat our homes, to cook our food, to use our computers. Everything we do requires energy and fossil fuels are a great source of energy. What is a fossil fuel?

A fossil fuel is a fuel that was formed many hundreds of millions of years ago before the time of the dinosaurs--that's why they're called *fossil* fuels. Coal, oil, and natural gas are the three main forms of fossil fuels. They were formed during an age called the Carboniferous (kar-bon-IF-er-us) Period. "Carboniferous" gets its name from carbon, the basic element in coal and other fossil fuels. The Carboniferous Period occurred from about 360 to 286 million years ago. Today, we burn all three main types of fossil fuels for energy. But how did fossil fuels form and will they be around for us to use forever?

Swamps containing giant trees and other large leafy plants covered the Earth during the Carboniferous Period. Oceans, ponds, rivers and streams were filled with algae. (Algae is actually millions of very small plants.)

Eventually the plants and trees died and fell to the bottom of the seas and swamps where they formed layers of a material called peat. Hundreds of years passed, during which the peat became covered by sand and clay and other minerals. The sand, clay, and other minerals turned into a type of rock called sedimentary.

Layers and layers of more and more rock piled up. The weight was enormous. The rock weighed down on the peat which was squeezed and squeezed until the water came out of it. Over millions and millions of years, that weighted down peat turned into oil, natural gas, and coal.

Fossil fuels are great for producing energy, however there is a limited amount of them and once they are all gone, they are gone forever. We cannot make any more oil, natural gas or coal; it took hundreds of millions of years to create the fossil fuels we use today. Fossil fuels are a finite resource. (Finite, which means "having limits," is the opposite of infinite, which means "without limits.") There is a limit to the amount of fossil fuels we have. If we run out of all fossil fuels, we will have to find another way to make energy. It is very important to discover new means of creating energy so that we do not have to rely entirely on fossil fuels. And of course, it is very important to conserve energy and thereby conserve fossil fuels so they will be around for years to come. Remember, you never know how much you'll miss something until it's gone.

1. The author's general purpose in this passage is to:
    a. persuade
    b. inform
    c. entertain

2. Explain in your own words how fossil fuels were formed.

_____

_____

_____

3. According to the passage, how long ago was the Carboniferous Period?

    a.   about 360 to 286 million years ago

    b.   about 100 to 50 million years ago

    c.   about 560 million years ago

    d.   about 10-26 million years ago

4. In your own words, explain what the author probably meant by the last sentence?

_____

_____

_____

5. How would you probably feel if you discovered an infinite source of energy?

    a.   excited

    b.   alarmed

    c.   embarrassed

    d.   confused

Part G - Bonus

The bonus word for this lesson is **idiom**.

Idiom is pronounced: ID ee uhm

Idiom is a phrase or expression in which words are used in a special way that is different from their literal meaning. Each language has its own unique set of **idioms**.

An example of an **idiom** is: "hitch your wagon to the stars."

This saying is not about wagons and stars. Rather, it means "set your goals very high."

The word **idiom** comes from a Greek word meaning "peculiar."

Lesson 22

Part A - Text Organization

Directions: Read the paragraph below, and then follow the instructions.

At the beginning of World War II, the United States Marines realized that the Japanese could break the communications code the Marines were using. The Marines, therefore, were faced with the difficult challenge of finding a code that the enemy could not break. They eventually found the solution to their problem on the Navajo Reservation. The Navajo language was chosen because it was an unwritten language known only to the Navajo people. The language is complicated, and words are hard to pronounce. While on the reservation, the Marines recruited young men who became known as the code talkers. The code talkers developed and used codes in their native language to send secret messages for the Marines. The plan worked, and the Japanese were never able to break the Navajo code.

1. Circle the text that goes in box #1 in the diagram below.
2. What is a good heading for box #2 in the diagram below?

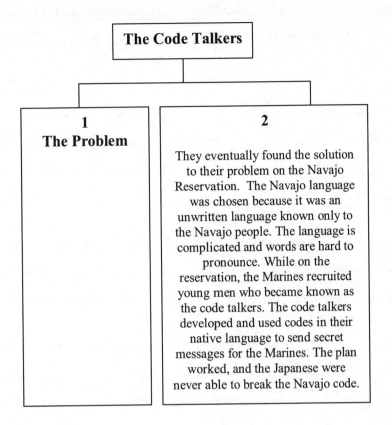

Part B - Author's Purpose

Directions: In the passage below from Lesson 21, the author's *general* purpose is to persuade the reader that sleep is important. After re-reading the passage, choose a statement of the author's main *specific* purpose.

We live in a world that requires A LOT of energy. We need energy to make our cars run, to heat our homes, to cook our food, to use our computers. Everything we do requires energy and fossil fuels are a great source of energy. What is a fossil fuel?

A fossil fuel is a fuel that was formed many hundreds of millions of years ago before the time of the dinosaurs--that's why they're called *fossil* fuels. Coal, oil, and natural gas are the three main forms of fossil fuels. They were formed during an age called the Carboniferous (kar-bon-IF-er-us) Period. "Carboniferous" gets its name from carbon, the basic element in coal and other fossil fuels. The Carboniferous Period occurred from about 360 to 286 million years ago. Today, we burn all three main types of fossil fuels for energy. But how did fossil fuels form and will they be around for us to use forever?

Swamps containing giant trees and other large leafy plants covered the Earth during the Carboniferous Period. Oceans, ponds, rivers and streams were filled with algae. (Algae is actually millions of very small plants.)

Eventually the plants and trees died and fell to the bottom of the seas and swamps where they formed layers of a material called peat. Hundreds of years passed, during which the peat became covered by sand and clay and other minerals. The sand, clay, and other minerals turned into a type of rock called sedimentary.

Layers and layers of more and more rock piled up. The weight was enormous. The rock weighed down on the peat which was squeezed and squeezed until the water came out of it. Over millions and millions of years, that weighted down peat turned into oil, natural gas, and coal.

Fossil fuels are great for producing energy, however there is a limited amount of them and once they are all gone, they are gone forever. We cannot make any more oil, natural gas or coal; it took hundreds of millions of years to create the fossil fuels we use today. Fossil fuels are a finite resource. (Finite, which means "having limits," is the opposite of infinite, which means "without limits.") There is a limit to the amount of fossil fuels we have. If we run out of all fossil fuels, we will have to find another way to make energy. It is very important to discover new means of creating energy so that we do not have to rely entirely on fossil fuels. And of course, it is very important to conserve energy and thereby conserve fossil fuels so they will be around for years to come. Remember, you never know how much you'll miss something until it's gone.

1. Which of the following sentences expresses the author's specific purpose?

   a. The author's purpose is to persuade the reader that fossil fuels are important for energy production and should be conserved.

   b. The author's purpose is to entertain the reader with a story about dinosaurs.

   c. The author's purpose is to persuade the reader that fossil fuels came from plants.

   d. The author's purpose is to persuade readers that we need to find a way to make more fossil fuels.

Part C - Main Idea

Directions: Re-read the passage above in Part B. Put an *X* beside the *three* phrases that just tell details from the passage. Write *GT* next to the phrase that would be a good title for the passage.

a. _____ What is a Yawn Trying to Tell You?

b. _____ Your Brain Has Connections

c. _____ Sleep Can Be Learning's Best Friend

d. _____ Why Teenagers Need More Sleep

Part D - Word Meaning

Directions: After you read each model, choose the best possible meaning for the underlined word.

1. **Model**: These new connections help <u>boost</u> memory, concentration, creativity, and learning.

    a. increase

    b. develop

2. **Model**: The <u>flagrant</u> snoring of the person sitting next to me during the movie ruined my evening.

    a. impossible to ignore

    b. brief

Part E - Review

Directions: Read the passage below and then answer the questions.

During the industrial age, America gained many new wealthy people. The author Mark Twain used the term "The Gilded Age" to describe the new showy culture that was similar to that of upper-class Europeans. It was a time of enormous mansions filled with expensive art work, antiques, and rare books. Wealthy people's free time was spent enjoying operas or going to luxurious resorts. They attended or took part in any activity that they believed showed signs of elegance.

At the time, most Americans led a far different lifestyle. The middle class believed in the value of hard work, but they also took time to relax. They enjoyed fairs where they could view the latest machines and inventions that showed progress toward more efficient production of goods. They eagerly attended circuses and sporting events. Baseball grew so popular after 1900 that it was called the national pastime. The newest kinds of entertainment attracting attention were the motion picture and records played on phonographs. The most popular reading materials were those that focused on adventure, courage, and the value of hard work.

1. The author's general purpose in this passage is to:

    a.   persuade

    b.   inform

    c.   entertain

2. During the age of growth in America, most Americans still believed in the value of:

    a.   hard work

    b.   entertainment

    c.   vacations

    d.   making money

3. The author responsible for the phrase "The Gilded Age" was:

    a.   Horatio Alger

    b.   Andrew Carnegie

    c.   Mark Twain

    d.   Eli Whitney

4. In your own words, briefly describe the differences between wealthy and middle class people during "The Gilded Age."

_____

_____

_____

5. In the 1900's, what became known as the national pastime?

    a.   listening to records on a phonograph

    b.   visiting resorts for vacations

    c.   going to baseball games

    d.   going to county and state fairs

Part F - Bonus

Remember, an **idiom** is a phrase or expression in which words are used in a special way that is different from their literal meaning. Each language has its own unique set of **idioms**.

An example of an **idiom** is "loose cannon."

If a cannon on a ship came loose, it could move around the deck causing unpredictable damage. Today, a "loose cannon" is anything unpredictable, and usually likely to do some damage.

BONUS REVIEW

A **cognitive map** is a representation of someone's thinking. When you read, a **cognitive map** represents the author's thinking. When you write, you can use a **cognitive map** to organize your own thinking.

The word **cognitive** comes from Greek.

Lesson 23

Part A - Text Organization

Directions: Read the paragraph below, and then follow the instructions.

Lake Chad used to be the largest freshwater lake in northern Africa. Forty years ago it was larger than the state of Vermont. Today, it is only half the size of the state of Rhode Island!

Where did the water go? Researchers have found that people and nature have both had a hand in the disappearance of the lake. Because the lake is shallow, the water level has always gone up and down. A lot of water evaporates during the dry season, so the lake shrinks. It rises when the monsoon rains fall in the mountains, and the runoff travels down the rivers until it reaches the lake.   For about 40 years the monsoon rains have been less than normal. About 20 years ago, water was taken from the rivers for farming. Both these factors have contributed to the decreasing water level in Lake Chad.

1. Fill in the blank oval in the diagram below.
2. Fill in the empty box in the diagram below.

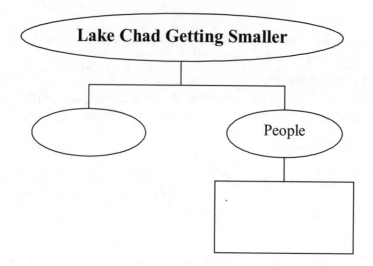

Part B - Author's Purpose

Directions: In the passage below, the author's *general* purpose is to persuade the reader into thinking a certain way. After reading the passage, choose a statement of the author's main *specific* purpose.

Police are always faced with the possibility of trying to control protestors who may become violent. In one state, law enforcement officers are urging legislators to make it a felony to intentionally hurt a police horse.

Harming a police dog is a felony which may carry a penalty of up to one year in jail. A bill was introduced in the United States House of Representatives to have the same penalty apply to hurting a police horse. These are not just horses; they are also considered police officers' partners, as well as an important part of the police force.

These horses can weigh more than 1,000 pounds, but people still try to hurt them. Police horses have been pelted with rocks and bottles, punched, bitten, kicked, and cut with a razor. Animal abuse laws currently aren't strong enough to protect police horses.

Police horses deserve the same protection and respect as police dogs. There are currently no federal laws to stop the abuse of police horses. This is a serious problem that needs to be underline{addressed} for the safety of everyone involved.

1. Which of the following sentences expresses the author's specific purpose?

   a. The author's purpose is to persuade the reader that police horses face the same dangers as police dogs.

   b. The author's purpose is to inform the reader about the duties of a police horse.

   c. The author's purpose is to persuade the reader that a federal law needs to be put into place that protects police horses because of their importance to police departments.

   d. The author's purpose is to persuade the reader to respect all members of the police department, including dogs and horses.

Part C - Main Idea

Directions: Re-read the passage above in Part B. Put an X beside the *three* statements that just tell details from the passage. Place the letters *MI* next to the statement that is a good main idea statement.

   a. _____ Police horses are effective in crowd control because of their size.

   b. _____ A partnership develops between a police officer and her police horse.

   c. _____ Harming a police dog may carry a fine of up to one year in jail.

   d. _____ Police horses play an important role in the police department, and need to be protected from harm by law.

Part D - Word Meaning

Directions: After you read each model, choose the best possible meaning for the underlined word.

1. **Model:** This is a serious problem that needs to be addressed for the safety of everyone involved.

   a. labeled

   b. given attention

2. **Model:** The representative's predecessor was interested in the law, but was not elected again.

   a. one who came before

   b. one who comes after

Part E - Review

Directions: Read the passage below and then answer the questions.

As countries became industrialized, child labor became a serious problem. Many children under the age of 10 were employed by factories, mills, and mines. These children worked long hours in dangerous and unhealthy conditions. Many times, the jobs they performed required the strength of an adult. The factories, mills, and mines were dirty and poorly lit. If the children became tired, an "over looker" would make sure they stayed awake.

Children could be paid lower wages than adults, and they were less likely to cause trouble. The small, nimble fingers of children were perfect for running the machines in factories. Orphans were often forced into these jobs.

As the textile industry developed in America, 40 per cent of all factory workers in New England were between the ages of 7 and 16. Over time, laws were passed to protect children working in factories. One law kept children under the age of 15 out of the factories unless they had attended school for at least three months the year before. Child labor laws were difficult to enforce for two reasons. One reason was that there were many poor families who needed the income their children could bring home. The second reason was that the government did not want to upset the factory owners by limiting child labor.

Laws have now been passed to make sure that the working conditions for children are not dangerous or unhealthy. These laws also set the age limit for getting a job, the number of daily and weekly hours a child can work, and the minimum hourly wage.

1. The author's general purpose of this passage is to:
    a. persuade
    b. inform
    c. entertain

2. Why would children be hired to work in factories?
    a. They could be paid lower wages.
    b. Their fingers were small and flexible enough to work the machines well.
    c. Children were less likely to cause trouble.
    d. All of the above.

3. Which word best describes how young children working in the factories probably felt?
    a. thankful
    b. fearful
    c. proud
    d. adventurous

4. Briefly explain the reasons for your answer to question # 3.

_____

_____

_____

5. What now protects children from the working conditions of the past?

    a.   child labor laws

    b.   an amendment to the Constitution

    c.   the Bill of Rights

    d.   a law that forbids children to work

6. The passage doesn't tell you the answer exactly, but why would a family send their child to work?

    a.   They didn't have baby-sitters to watch them while the parents were at work.

    b.   The families wanted their children to learn a skill early in life.

    c.   The family needed the extra income to pay for food, housing, and clothing.

    d.   The children could choose between going to school and working in the factories.

Part F - Bonus

Idiom is a phrase or expression in which words are used in a special way that is different from their literal meaning.

Idiom is pronounced:

   ID ee uhm

An example of an **idiom** is "There's more than one way to skin a cat."

We aren't sure where this saying came from. It might be a reference to taking the skin off of catfish, rather than the family pet!

The meaning of the saying is "there is more than one way to achieve a goal."

BONUS REVIEW

Anaphora means "a pronoun or other words used to refer to some other word or name." Pronouns are one type of **anaphora**. **Anaphora** comes from the Greek language. *Ana* means "up" and *pherein* means "carry" in Greek.

Lesson 24

Part A - Text Organization

Directions: Read the paragraph below from Lesson 21, and then follow the instructions.

An important incident occurred in the colonial city of Boston on March 5, 1770. It started with a few colonists tormenting a British soldier who was standing guard at the Customs House. The Boston colonists didn't like having British soldiers in their city. The lone soldier threatened the colonists, who in turn called more colonists to the scene. With that increased threat, the British soldier called for more help. A small group of soldiers under the leadership of Captain Thomas Preston came to the aid of the lone soldier. The colonists, in response, surrounded Captain Preston and his men. No one knows exactly what happened next, but a soldier fired his musket into the threatening crowd. Five colonists ended up dead and several other people were hurt. No matter how it started, the incident was tragic. Sam Adams, a cousin of the future President of the United States, John Adams, took advantage of the incident as a way to help rile up more colonists to support independence from the British. Adams gave the incident a name, which inspired many colonial patriots and remains famous to this day: The Boston Massacre.

1. Fill in the blank square in the diagram below.
2. Fill in the blank oval in the diagram below.

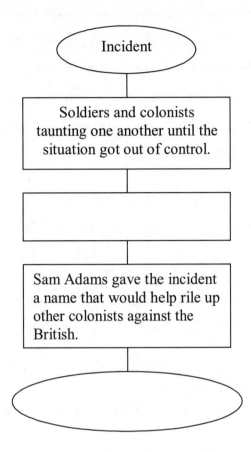

Part B - Author's Purpose

Directions: In the passage below from Lesson 23, the author's *general* purpose is to inform the reader about child labor during the industrial era. Re-read the passage, and then choose a statement of the author's main *specific* purpose.

As countries became industrialized, child labor became a serious problem. Many children under the age of 10 were employed by factories, mills, and mines. These children worked long hours in dangerous and unhealthy conditions. Many times, the jobs they performed required the strength of an adult. The factories, mills, and mines were dirty and poorly lit. If the children became tired, an "overlooker" would make sure they stayed awake.

Children could be paid lower wages than adults, and they were less likely to cause trouble. The small, nimble fingers of children were perfect for running the machines in factories. Orphans were often forced into these jobs.

Lesson 24

As the textile industry developed in America, 40 per cent of all factory workers in New England were between the ages of 7 and 16. Over time, laws were passed keeping children under the age of 15 out of the factories unless they had attended school for at least three months the year before. Any child labor law was difficult to enforce for two reasons. There were many poor families who needed the income their children could bring home, and the government did not want to upset the factory owners by limiting child labor.

Laws have now been passed to make sure the working conditions for children are not dangerous or unhealthy. These laws also set the age limit for getting a job, the number of daily and weekly hours a child can work, and the minimum hourly wage.

1. Which of the following sentences expresses the author's specific purpose?

   a. The author's purpose is to persuade the reader that society didn't care about the welfare of their children.

   b. The author's purpose is to inform the reader about the dreadful working conditions many children were forced into during the industrial age.

   c. The author's purpose is to inform the reader that children were good workers who seldom caused any trouble.

   d. The author's purpose is to inform the reader that there are now laws that regulate the working conditions of children.

Part C - Main Idea

Directions: Re-read the passage above in Part B. Put an X beside the *three* statements that just tell details from the passage. Place an S next to the statement that is a good summary statement of the passage.

   a. _____ Many orphaned children were forced to work at any early age.

   b. _____ Children often needed to work in order for their families to have enough money buy the things they needed.

   c. _____ Children made better workers than adults did in the mines and factories.

   d. _____ Before laws were passed for their protection, children were hired to work long hours, and were subjected to dirty and unsafe conditions.

Part D - Word Meaning

Directions: After you read each model, choose the best possible meaning for the underlined word.

1. **Model**: Before laws were passed for their protection, children were hired to work long hours and were <u>subjected</u> to dirty and unsafe conditions.

    a. exposed

    b. limited

2. **Model:** Any child labor law was difficult to <u>enforce</u> for two reasons.

    a. change

    b. carry out effectively

Part E- Review

Directions: Read the passage below and then answer the questions.

In 1889, Jane Addams used her own money to buy a run-down mansion in one of Chicago's worst slums. Known as Hull House, it was one of the first places to help disadvantaged people gain self-respect and begin to feel comfortable in society. Addams and other dedicated volunteers lived there and worked to improve conditions for the poor. Most of the people they helped were immigrants who had come to find work in the stockyards and steel mills. The project began with a day-care center. Soon there was also a kindergarten, a library, a theater, and Chicago's first public playground. Hull House expanded over the years until it filled 13 buildings and covered an entire city block.

Addams never seemed to grow tired of fighting for child-labor laws, an eight-hour workday, and the improvement of housing. Jane Addams and her friend, Ellen Gates Starr, made many speeches about the needs of poor neighborhoods, and raised money to take care of those needs. Together, they took care of children and those who were sick. Just as importantly, they listened to the troubles of people. Many people came to the center for weekly baths. Classes were even held during the evening for adults. By the second year, two thousand people a week were taking advantage of what Hull House had to offer.

Jane Addams fought to help gain women the right to vote. She also encouraged women to discover their ambitions, and to find opportunities to fulfill them. In 1931 Addams became the first American woman to win the Nobel Peace Prize.

1. The author's general purpose in this passage is to:

    a.   persuade

    b.   inform

    c.   entertain

2. Jane Addams was a person known as a *humanitarian*. Briefly explain, with details from the passage, the traits of a *humanitarian*.

    _____

    _____

    _____

3. Hull House was located in the city of:

    a.   New York

    b.   Boston

    c.   Chicago

    d.   St. Louis

4. The passage doesn't tell you, but Jane Addams' present day occupation would probably be:

    a.   a teacher who was teaching adults in night school

    b.   a nurse working in a hospital

    c.   a child care worker in a day-care center

    d.   a social worker who helped people with their problems

5. Which service did Hull House provide that perhaps *meant* the most and *cost* the least?

    a.   providing a place to bathe

    b.   listening to other's problems

    c.   giving speeches to help raise money

    d.   taking care of the sick

Part F - Bonus

Another example of an **idiom** is "Don't look a gift horse in the mouth."

You can generally tell how old or young a horse is by looking at its teeth. If someone were to give you a horse as a gift, it would be impolite to look in the horse's mouth to see how old it is.

The meaning of this saying is "don't be ungrateful or impolite when someone gives you a gift."

BONUS REVIEW

Inference means "guessing about something from another thing that you already know."   You have been answering many **inference** questions in this program.

Lesson 26

Part A - Summarize Passage

Directions: Read the passage, and then follow the directions.

After Henri got his allowance, he bought a new CD. He liked all the songs, but his favorites were the first and last songs. His sister didn't like any of the songs. She asked Henri to wear headphones when he played the CD.

Now look below at the summary list for this passage.

Summary List:
1.   Henri buys a CD with his allowance.
2.   He likes the first and last songs.
3.   His sister doesn't like any of the songs.
4.   She asks Henri to use headphones.

Finally, use the list to help you write a short summary of the passage, in your own words. A summary should be two or three sentences long.

_____

_____

_____

Reading Success | 99

Part B- Main Idea

Directions: Below are three statements that are details from the passage in Part A. After reading the details, write a statement that would make a good main idea statement for the passage. Part of the statement is already written for you.

His sister didn't like any of the songs.

His favorite songs were the first and the last ones.

Henri bought a new CD with his allowance.

Henri's sister asked him to wear headphone when listening to his CD because

Part C- Review

Read the passage and then answer the questions.

In the 1600's, horse-drawn wagons were used to haul goods locally. The poor conditions of roads made it almost impossible for them to be used for long hauls. Long distance transporting was done by horses plodding along the banks of rivers and canals, pulling boats and barges with ropes.

A canal is a waterway dug across land. Canal builders in Europe dug hundreds of canals from the late Middle Ages through the early 1800's. Canals have served as an important method of transporting goods for thousands of years. The first canals in Britain were built to carry coal cheaply from mines to industrial towns. Canals contributed to the Industrial Revolution by providing a better way of transporting raw materials and finished goods.

The Erie Canal was the first major American canal. It opened in New York in 1825, and connected the cities of Albany and Buffalo. The canal provided an all water route between New York City and the ports located on the Great Lakes. Before the Erie Canal opened, the journey over land between Albany and Buffalo took about 20 days. The same trip took only eight days using horses or mules to pull barges along the canal. After the success of the Erie Canal, the

United States entered into a whirlwind of canal building. By 1850, about 4,500 miles of canals had been built.

1. Which of the following sentences expresses the author's specific purpose?

   a. The author's purpose is to inform the reader about the importance of canals as a way to transport raw goods and finished products.

   b. The author's purpose is to persuade the reader that the Erie Canal was the most important canal in the world.

   c. The author's purpose is to inform the reader about the history of transporting goods.

   d. The author's purpose is to inform the reader about the use of horses as a method of transportation.

2. Which words in the passage tell you that the United States thought they needed to quickly build more canals?

   a. ...about 4,500 miles of canals had been built.

   b. ...entered into a whirlwind of canal building.

   c. Canals contributed to the Industrial Revolution...

   d. Europeans dug hundreds of canals...

3. Canal travel can **best** be described as a:

   a. good use of horses

   b. time-saver

   c. new invention

   d. way to use water

4. Put an X beside the three statements that just tell details from the passage. Write S next to the statement that is a summary of the passage.

   a. _____ Although canals have been used in some parts of the world for thousands of years, in America canals became an important method of transportation during the Industrialization Age.

   b. _____ The amount of time it took to transport goods by water was far less than it took to transport them by land.

   c. _____ Canals were used in Britain for many years before they appeared in the United States.

   d. _____ Connecting cities in the state of New York to the ports along the Great Lakes was important to manufacturers.

5. The first major canal in the United States was the:

   a. Suez Canal

   b. Panama Canal

   c. Erie Canal

   d. Cape Cod Canal

6. Which one of the following statements in an *opinion?*

    a. Horses and mules were the only animals used to pull the barges along the canals.

    b. The water in a canal is usually calmer than in lakes and oceans.

    c. Canal travel would probably not be the best form of transporting goods through mountains.

    d. Using horses to pull the barges along the canal was cruel treatment of the animals.

Part D- Text Organization

Directions: Read the paragraph in Part C, and then return to this section and follow the instructions.

1. Circle the text that should go in box #4 in the diagram below.

2. What would be a good heading for box # 5 in the diagram below?

_____

3. What would be a good heading for box #6 in the diagram below?

_____

1. Early Long Distance Transportation

2. Short Distance Transportation

In the 1600's, horse-drawn wagons were used to haul goods locally. The poor conditions of roads made it almost impossible for them to be used for long hauls.

3. Long Distance Transportation

Long distance transporting was done by horses plodding along the banks of rivers and canals, pulling boats and barges with ropes.

4. Canals

5.

The first canals in Britain were built to carry coal cheaply from mines to industrial towns. Canals contributed to the Industrial Revolution by providing a better way of transporting raw materials and finished goods.

6.

The Erie Canal was the first major American canal. It opened in New York in 1825, and connected the cities of Albany and Buffalo. The canal provided an all water route between New York City and the ports located on the Great Lakes. Before the Erie Canal opened, the journey over land between Albany and Buffalo took about 20 days. The same trip took only eight days using horses or mules to pull barges along the canal.

Part E - Bonus

Look at the beginning of a poem by Henry Wadsworth Longfellow:

The Fire of Drift-Wood

DEVEREUX FARM, NEAR MARBLEHEAD

1 We sat within the farm-house old,

2 Whose windows, looking o'er the bay,

3 Gave to the sea-breeze damp and cold,

4 An easy entrance, night and day.

5 Not far away we saw the port,

6 The strange, old-fashioned, silent town,

7 The lighthouse, the dismantled fort,

8 The wooden houses, quaint and brown.

Lines 1-4 are the first **stanza**. Lines 5-8 are the second **stanza**. A **stanza** is usually at least four lines long. A poet might simply write the lines and group them together. But the lines of a **stanza** might stand together in at least two other ways:

1. they might stand together in one **rhyme pattern**
2. they might stand together because they express one main idea, like a paragraph

Stanza comes from the Latin word *stare* (STAR ay) which means to "stand." There are many English words that come from *stare*, such as stand, stagnant, state, and static. There are also many other words that have *stare* in them like constant, distant, and substance.

Both of the **stanzas** above have the same **rhyming pattern**. The first and third lines rhyme in the first stanza and the second stanza, and the second and fourth lines rhyme, too, in both stanzas.

The **rhyming pattern** for both stanzas is a b a b.

That is a short way of showing a **rhyming pattern**.

BONUS REVIEW

A **cognitive map** is a representation of someone's thinking. It could represent your thinking when you write, or the thinking of the author when you read. **Cognitive** comes from Greek.

The characters in **fables** are usually animals, plants, or even objects such as rocks. These characters talk, and think, and generally act like people.

Lesson 27

Part A - Summarize Passage

Directions: Read the passage, and then follow the directions.

Blue moon is a folklore term that has several possible sources. As early as 1528, this term was used to mean "a foolish belief." There are rare examples of the moon actually appearing blue after volcanic eruptions or unusual weather conditions. Another possible source is from The Maine Farmers' Almanac. Very rarely, there are two full moons in a calendar month. When this occurred, the almanac printed the date of the first full moon in red and the date of the second in blue. Today, people usually refer to uncommon events, or events that don't happen very often, as occurring "once in a blue moon."

Now look below at the summary list for this passage.

Summary List:
1. The term "blue moon" is a folklore term.
2. In early times, the term meant a foolish belief.
3. The moon may actually appear blue after volcanic eruptions or unusual weather conditions.
4. The *Maine Farmers' Almanac* printed the first full moon in red and the second in blue if there were two full moons in the same month.
5. Later, people described uncommon events as occurring "once in a blue moon."

Finally, use the list to help you write a short summary of the passage, in your own words. A summary should be two or three sentences long.

_____

_____

_____

_____

Part B- Text Organization

Directions: Using information from the paragraph above, follow the instructions.

1. Fill in the blank rectangle in the first row of boxes in the diagram below.
2. Fill in the two blank rectangles in the second row of the diagram below.

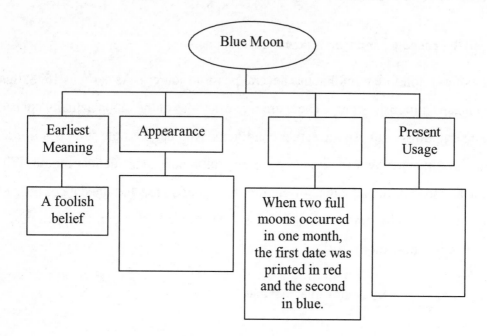

Part C - Main Idea

Directions: Below are three statements that are details from the passage in Part A. After reading the details, write a statement that would make a good main idea statement for the passage. Part of the statement is already written for you.

Every once in a while, two full moons will occur in the same month.

A farmer's almanac would print the first full moon in red and the second full moon in blue.

The meaning of the term "blue moon" is based in folklore.

The meaning of the phrase "blue moon"

_____

_____

Part D - Review

Directions: Read the passage and then answer the questions.

Buying clothes in the store seems like a pretty easy, and most often enjoyable, task. But, did you ever stop to think about the actual process it takes to turn raw material, such as cotton, into a shirt or pair of socks?

The fuzzy strands of cotton fiber need to be spun into yarn. The yarn can then be woven into cloth. English inventors developed machines that could spin cotton much faster than ever before. In fact, with these new machines, workers could spin cotton fiber into yarn much faster than the weavers could turn the yarn into cloth.

One day, a weaver by the name of James Hargreaves watched his daughter, Jenny, accidently knock over the family spinning wheel. The spindle continued to revolve. Seeing this gave him the idea that a whole line of spindles could be made to revolve from one wheel. Hargreaves built a machine using eight spindles onto which thread was spun. By turning a single wheel, eight threads could be spun at once. Later, improvements were made so that the "spinning jenny" could handle 80 threads at once.

By now, the spinners and the weavers couldn't get enough cotton fiber. An American, Eli Whitney, was the inventor of the cotton gin. The cotton gin was able to separate the cotton fiber from the seeds. This work was usually done by hand, but the cotton gin made it much faster and more efficient. Therefore, the need for the cotton fiber could be filled at a faster rate.

1. Which of the following sentences expresses the author's specific purpose?

    a. The author's purpose is to inform the reader about the uses of spinning wheels.

    b. The author's purpose is to inform the reader about separating the cotton seeds from the fiber.

    c. The author's purpose is to inform the reader about the inventions of the "spinning jenny" and the cotton gin, and their uses in manufacturing cloth.

    d. The author's purpose is to persuade the reader that the cotton gin was an important invention to clothing manufacturers.

2. Which event happened *last*?

    a.   Eli Whitney invented the cotton gin.

    b.   Spinners and weavers couldn't get enough cotton fiber.

    c.   James Hargreaves invented the "spinning jenny."

    d.   Jenny Hargreaves knocked over the family spinning wheel.

3. What is the job of the weavers?

    a.   separate the cotton seed from the fiber

    b.   spin the fibers into yarn

    c.   turn yarn into cloth

    d.   color the cloth

4. There is enough information in this passage to show that:

    a.   New ideas can sometimes be the result of something simple happening.

    b.   If there is a need for something that will make work more efficient, an invention may soon follow to fill that need.

    c.   Many times one invention leads to another invention.

    d.   All of the above.

5. The inspiration for James Hargreaves' invention took place:

    a.   in a factory

    b.   at his home

    c.   at an inventors convention

    d.   from reading a book on weaving

6. Using information from the passage, briefly describe in your own words the three steps in making cloth from cotton.

_____

_____

_____

Part E - Bonus

Here are the first two stanzas of a Longfellow poem:

a We sat within the farm-house old,

b Whose windows, looking o'er the bay,

a Gave to the sea-breeze damp and cold,

b An easy entrance, night and day.

a Not far away we saw the port,

b The strange, old-fashioned, silent town,

a The lighthouse, the dismantled fort,

b The wooden houses, quaint and brown.

This clearly shows the **rhyming pattern** of both **stanzas** of the poem.

a, old

b, bay

a, cold

b, day

a, port

b, town

a, fort

b, brown

BONUS REVIEW

An example of an **idiom** is "bad hair day."

This demonstrates a rare case when a line from a movie turns into a widely used **idiom**. The movie was "Buffy the Vampire Slayer," first shown in 1992.

The meaning is "one of those days when everything seems to go wrong."

Lesson 28

Part A - Summarize Passage

Directions: Read the passage, and then follow the directions.

A bibliography is a list of books and articles. You can find a bibliography at the end of many books, magazines articles, or reports. A bibliography tells the reader exactly where the writer got his or her information. Certain kinds of information are supplied in a bibliography: authors, titles, editions, and date and place of publication, for example. The bibliography can also lead the reader to other sources that relate to a particular subject. Say, for example, you were doing a report on constellations and your first source of information was a magazine article. At the end of the magazine article there would be a list of the sources the author used in gathering information about constellations for the article. Those sources would also have bibliographies that would lead you to even more sources.

Now look below at the summary list for this passage.

Summary List:
1. A bibliography is a list of books and magazine articles.
2. A bibliography can be found at the end of books, magazines articles, or reports.
3. Where a writer found her information can be found in a bibliography.
4. A bibliography can also lead the reader to other sources of information about a particular subject.

Finally, use the list to help you write a short summary of the passage, in your own words.
A summary should be two or three sentences long.

_____

_____

_____

_____

Part B - Text Organization

A Venn diagram is another way to organize important information comparing two things. Areas 1 and 2 list details showing how the two ideas are *different*. The area where the circles overlap lists a detail that is *common* to both ideas.

Directions: Fill in boxes 1, 2, and 3.

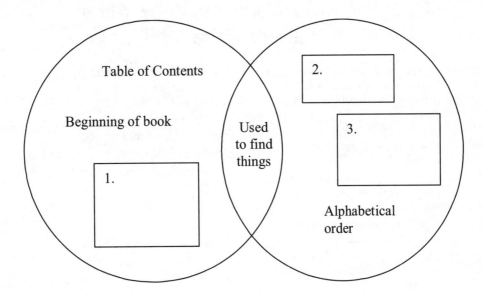

Part C - Main Idea

Directions: Below are three statements that are details from the passage in Part A. After reading the details, write a statement that would make a good main idea statement for the passage. Part of the statement is already written for you.

A bibliography can be used as a way to find more information about a subject.

A bibliography can be found at the end of books, magazine articles, or reports.

Entries in a bibliography are listed in alphabetical order.

A bibliography lists sources

_____

_____

Part D - Review

Directions: Read the passage and then answer the question.

Everything You Wanted to Know About Laissez-Faire

- Individuals should be free to make their own decisions about what to make and how much to charge for them.
- Don't let the government decide how employers should treat their employees.
- Banks should be free to decide the amount of interest they will charge.
- Goods from other countries should not be heavily taxed.
- Do away with monopolies. All companies should be free to trade with other parts of the world.

- Get motivated to try new ideas. The harder you work the more money you'll make.
- Get involved in inventing, manufacturing and trading products.
- As a result all of our society will become richer.

Ideas taken from the book: *"The Wealth of Nations"* by Adam Smith.

I agree with many of the statements in the book *The Wealth of Nations*. There has been an unfortunate side to the laissez-faire movement, however. My employer is a huge fan of laissez-faire. Why? It's because the government has no say in how he runs his business. We are now right back where we started with the unsafe and unsanitary working conditions. My employer no longer has to care about how many hours we work, or the wages we get paid. I have, however, seen the positive side of laissez-faire in the new inventions and the investments others are making. Some people are definitely making more money. But, the idea of "to let alone" works much better for the employer than it does for the employee.

1. Which of the following sentences expresses the author's specific purpose?

    a. The author's purpose is to explain to the reader the benefits and drawbacks of the laissez-faire policy.

    b. The author's purpose is to persuade the reader that the less government is involved, the better.

    c. The author's purpose is to inform the reader about Adam Smith.

    d. The author's purpose is to persuade the reader that inventing and manufacturing is the way to make them richer.

2. Adam Smith wrote a book titled:

    a.   *The Laissez-faire Way to a Richer Life*

    b.   *Using Your Imagination to Invent*

    c.   *The Wealth of Nations*

    d.   *Understanding What Laissez-faire Really Means*

3. Briefly describe how the author probably feels about the beliefs of Adam Smith.

_____

_____

_____

4. Which idiom best describes this passage?

    a.   Money is the root of all evil.

    b.   There are two sides to every coin.

    c.   Rome wasn't built in a day.

    d.   A friend in need is a friend indeed.

5. Which words from the passage mean the same as "laissez-faire?"

    a.   ...the idea of "to let alone"

    b.   ...our society will become richer

    c.   Get involved...

    d.   The harder you work...

Part E - Bonus

A poet might simply write the lines of a **stanza** and group them together. But the lines of a **stanza** might stand together in at least two other ways:

1. they might stand together in one **rhyme scheme**
2. they might stand together because they express one main idea, like a paragraph.

Stanza comes from the Latin word *stare* (STAR ay) which means to "stand."

BONUS REVIEW

Literal is pronounced like this:

    LIT•er•ul

Literal comes from the Latin word *littera* (LIT er ah), which means "letter" or "word."

When you take a reading test, some of the questions you have to answer are **literal** questions. That means that you can find the answer to the questions in the passage you are reading.

Lesson 29

Part A - Summarize Passage

Directions: Read the passage, and then follow the directions.

Desert animals have a way of adapting to the heat and lack of rain in their surroundings. Some of these ways can be quite fascinating. To reach water, the acacia tree sends its roots down over one hundred feet. Cactus leaves are reduced to thin spines to cut down on water loss. Many desert animals don't actually drink water, but get it from the foods they eat. Others, like the camel, can go for many days without water. A jackrabbit keeps cool by using its ears. Their ears are tall and thin, and provide a large surface area for releasing heat.

Now look below at the summary list for this passage.

Summary List:
1. Desert animals adapt to the heat and lack of rain.
2. Some trees send down roots hundreds of feet in order to reach water.
3. Other plants have small thin leaves that cut down on evaporation.
4. Some animals get their water from the foods they eat, while other animals don't need to drink much water.
5. A jackrabbit keeps cool by releasing body heat through its large ears.

Finally, use the list to help you write a short summary of the passage, in your own words. A summary should be two or three sentences long.

_____

_____

_____

_____

Part B - Text Organization

Directions: Using information from the paragraph above, follow the instructions.

1. Fill in the first blank square at the top of the diagram below.
2. Fill in the blank rectangle on the left hand side of the diagram below.
3. Fill in the blank rectangle on the right hand side of the diagram below.
4. Fill in the blank triangle in the diagram below.

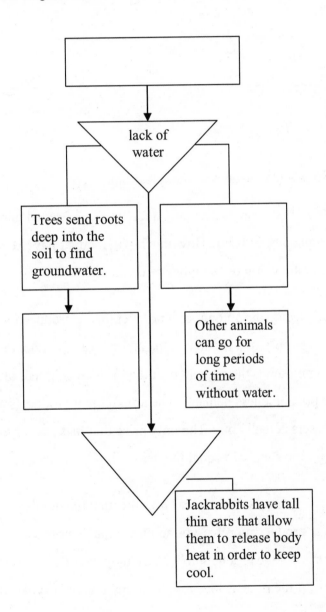

Part C - Main Idea

Directions: Below are three statements that are details from the passage in Part A. After reading the details, write a statement that would make a good main idea statement for the passage.

To survive in the desert, certain trees send roots hundreds of feet deep to find ground water.

Some animals get the water they need from the food they eat.

Cactus leaves are reduced to thin spines to cut down on water loss.

Part D - Review

Directions: Read the passage and then answer the questions.

During the Industrial Age, there were many questions that needed to be answered. For example: What will people buy and sell? How much will a buyer pay? How much profit can a seller make? Welcome to the <u>world</u> of "supply and demand."

Supply and demand decide the amount of a product that is produced and the price people are willing to pay for it. The **supply** of a product is the amount of a product that businesses offer for sale. The **demand** for a product is the amount of it that users would like to buy, at a certain price. Usually, the higher the price, the less demand. The amount that producers actually sell **must equal** the amount that users actually buy. The only price that makes everyone happy is the price that makes it possible for the supply to equal the demand.

Use the market for yo-yos as an example. From the manufacturer's point of view, higher prices encourage them to produce more yo-yos so they'll make more money with each sale. If the price is too low, it will discourage production because they won't make as much money. From the customer's point of view, if the price is low, they will buy lots of yo-yos. At high prices, the customers will buy other toys.

If the price is agreeable to the buyer and the seller, suppliers will offer just the amount of yo-yos that customers will buy. Supply will equal the demand. Everyone is happy.

If the price is higher than people want to pay, the stores will be full of yo-yos that no one wants to buy. If the price is too low, all the yo-yos are snatched up and there aren't any left. When the demand for yo-yos becomes higher than the supply, the price can rise again.

1. Which of the following sentences expresses the author's specific purpose?

    a. The author's purpose is to inform the reader that the more people want something, the more they will pay for it.

    b. The author's purpose is to explain to the reader that supply and demand is determined by price, profit, and priorities.

    c. The author's purpose is to inform the reader about the profit manufacturers make from the goods they sell.

    d. The author's purpose is to persuade the reader not to buy what he or she wants if it is too expensive.

2. According to the passage, when does the supply equal the demand?

    a. when the buyer pays a fair price for an item and the manufacturer makes as many items as needed while still being able to make a profit

    b. when the buyer is finally able to buy what he wants no matter what price he had to pay

    c. when the seller sets the price lower than another seller and all his supply is bought out quickly

    d. when the buyer thinks he is getting a good deal by buying things that are on sale

3. Which of the following statements would **most likely** be an example of the demand being higher than the supply.

    a. ordering something from the sale catalog

    b. having to get in line the night before tickets go on sale for a popular music concert

    c. buying half price movie tickets

    d. getting a "two for one" deal on books

4. Explain what would probably happen in a company that made school uniforms if every school decided to wear them. (Be sure to use the words supply and demand.)

_____

_____

_____

_____

5. Look at the underlined word in the model sentence. Then choose the sentence that uses the underlined word in the same way as the model sentence.

   Model: Welcome to the <u>world</u> of "supply and demand."

   a. The <u>world</u> of sports has become a game of dollars and cents.

   b. By being late for dinner and not calling ahead, I was in for a <u>world</u> of trouble.

   c. The <u>world</u> would be a better place if everyone was more accepting of the opinions of others.

   d. The planet earth is often referred to as the "<u>world</u>."

Use the bar graph below to answer questions 6 & 7.

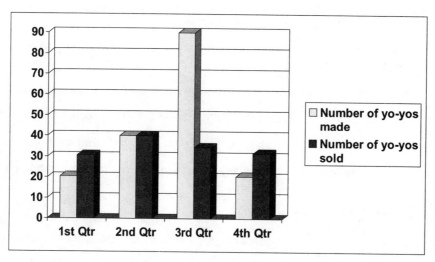

Jolly Yo-Yo Yearly Sales Report

6. In which quarter shown in the bar graph does the supply equal the demand?

   a. 4th Quarter

   b. 1st Quarter

   c. 2nd Quarter

   d. 3rd Quarter

7. In which quarter could the buyer expect to pay a lower than normal price?

   a. 3rd Quarter

   b. 1st Quarter

   c. 2nd Quarter

   d. 4th Quarter

Part E - Bonus

Read this brief verse:

> There isn't a day,
>
> I don't hear you say,
>
> "I'm off to the races,
>
> In adventurous places."

The **rhyming pattern** of this stanza is a a b b.

BONUS REVIEW

Anaphora means "a pronoun or other words used to refer to some other word or name." Pronouns are one type of **anaphora**. **Anaphora** comes from the Greek language. *Ana* means "up" and *pherein* means "carry" in Greek.

Lesson 31

Part A - Poetry

Here are the first two stanzas of a well known poem by Edgar Allen Poe, entitled "The Raven."

<u>Stanza 1</u>

> Once upon a midnight dreary, while I pondered weak and weary,
>
> Over many a quaint and curious volume of forgotten lore,
>
> While I nodded, nearly napping, suddenly there came a tapping,
>
> As of some one gently rapping, rapping at my chamber door.
>
> `'Tis some visitor,' I muttered, `tapping at my chamber door -
>
> Only this, and nothing more.'

<u>Stanza 2</u>

> Ah, distinctly I remember it was in the bleak December,
>
> And each separate dying ember wrought its ghost upon the floor.
>
> Eagerly I wished the morrow; - vainly I had sought to borrow
>
> From my books surcease of sorrow -sorrow for the lost Lenore -

For the rare and radiant maiden whom the angels named Lenore

Nameless here for evermore.

Usually, in order to understand poems, you have to read them more carefully than other types of writing. Here are some things you need to do to understand a poem:

1. Make sure you know what all the words mean.

    In stanza 1, "quaint" means "old fashioned but charming."

    "Lore" means "information about traditions or beliefs."

    In stanza 2, "wrought" is an old fashioned way of saying "worked."

    "Surcease" is related closely to the word "cease" and means "stop."

2. Look carefully at word order.

3. Look for hints about the setting of the poem.

4. Look for figurative language. For example, the line "...each separate dying ember wrought its ghost upon the floor" contains figurative language.

Part B - Poetry

Directions: Answer the questions about the section of "The Raven" presented in Part A.

1. You can tell just by reading the first two stanzas of this poem that the mood of the poem is grim. List at least two words that contribute to that mood.

    _____

2. At what time of day does this poem take place?

    _____

3. What time of year does the poem take place?

    _____

4. What was the narrator doing when the knocking at the door began?

    _____

5. Which lines in both stanzas rhyme?

    _____

Part C- Summarize Passage

Directions: Read the passage and then follow the directions.

Many years ago, to keep factory machines running and in good repair, men, women, and children worked many hours a day, six days a week. The working conditions were poor and wages were low.

In order to improve the working conditions, organizations called labor unions were formed. Many workers joined these unions and demanded better pay and safer working conditions. What happened if these demands were not met by the owners? Many of the workers refused to return to work by going on strike. If enough workers went on strike, they could close down entire companies. If the companies were shut down, then perhaps the owners would meet their demands.

Sometimes, the owners would give in to the workers' demands. Other times, they responded with force and violence. Eventually, labor unions and owners found non-violent ways to settle their differences.

Now look below at the summary list for this passage.

Summary List:

1. Men, women, and children worked many hours a week in the factories, many times under unsafe conditions.
2. Labor unions were formed to improve conditions and increase pay.
3. Sometimes, the demands of the workers were met.
4. Sometimes, owners would use violence against the workers.

Finally, use the list to help you write a short summary of the passage, in your own words. A summary should be two or three sentences long.

_____

_____

_____

_____

Part D - Main Idea

Directions: Below is the main idea statement for the passage in Part C. Write a detail from the passage that supports the main idea statement.

Labor Unions were organized to protect the rights of the workers, but violence often resulted when workers' demands were not met.

_____

_____

_____

Part E - Review

Directions: Read the passage and then answer the questions.

In the United States, Labor Day is a holiday dedicated to working people. There is some doubt about who first came up with the idea of a workers' holiday, but on the first Monday in September, we show support for workers and honor them for their achievements.

Whoever created the idea, Labor Day was first celebrated in New York City with a parade on September 5, 1882. In 1884 the holiday was moved to the first Monday in September. By 1885, similar celebrations were being held across the country. Oregon was the first state to make Labor Day a legal holiday in 1887. It finally became a national holiday in June 1894.

Labor Day is celebrated with parades, picnics, sporting events, and meetings of labor groups. The weekend that proceeds Labor Day is a popular part of the holiday as well, usually meaning there is one last chance to get out and enjoy the summer season.

The United States is not the only country that dedicates a day to honor workers. Canada and Puerto Rico celebrate Labor Day on the same day as the United States. Many other countries, including Guinea-Bissau and Honduras, celebrate a labor holiday on May 1.

1. Choose the best meaning for the underlined word in the model sentence

    Model: The weekend that <u>precedes</u> Labor Day is a popular part of the holiday as well, usually meaning there is one last chance to get out and enjoy the summer season.

    a. follows

    b. having the warmest temperatures

    c. comes right before

    d. occurs the week before

2. Why would the weekend preceding the Labor Day holiday signal the end of summer?

    _____

    _____

    _____

Using the information from the passage, follow the directions.

Labor Day Celebrations Change Throughout History

	Moved to the first Monday in September	Labor Day celebrations held across the land	Oregon first able to make Labor Day a holiday	
1882	1884		1887	1894

3. According to the information provided in the passage, fill in the date on the chart that would come between 1884 and 1887 on a timeline of Labor Day events.

4. Fill in the information from the passage that would match up with the year 1882.

5. Choose the best title for the passage, which would go in the top box.

    a. Labor Day Celebrates the Workers of America

    b. Time Brings Changes

    c. Labor Day Celebrations Change Through History

    d. Oregon Leads the Way in Labor Day Holiday

Part F - Bonus

Look at the line below from "The Raven." Pay special attention to the "accent marks."

> While´ I nod´ded, near´ly nap´ping, sud´denly´ there came´ a tap´ping,

The syllables in this line are accented in a structured way.

First, there are eight accented syllables in the line, indicated with the small ´ mark.

There are also eight unaccented, or weakly accented, syllables in the line, each one following an accented syllable. The syllables can be divided up like this:

> While´ I | nod´ded, | near´ly | nap´ping, | sud´den | ly´ there | came´ a | tap´ping,

In poetry, each division like this is called a **metrical foot**. Each "foot" in this line from "The Raven" is called a **trochee** (pronounced TROH key), which is a noun. The adjective form is **trochaic** (pronounced troh KAY ic). A **trochaic metrical foot** has one accented syllable, followed by one unaccented syllable. Each of the following words could be a **trochaic foot** in a poem:

> mo´ther o´pen af´ter snow´man sec´ond   ar´my blos´som

BONUS REVIEW

An example of an **idiom** is "break a leg."

When you want someone to do well during a performance, why would you say, "break a leg," when you are really wishing them good luck? No one knows the origin of this **idiom** for certain. Perhaps at one time, people were superstitious about wishing someone good luck, thinking that to do so might create bad luck. Therefore, maybe wishing someone bad luck (break a leg) might cause good luck. That is certainly a superstitious idea.

The meaning of the **idiom** "break a leg" is "good luck."

Lesson 32

Part A - Poetry

In the first two stanzas of Poe's "The Raven," a narrator is alone in his "chamber," which usually means a bedroom. He is trying to read some books, as a distraction from his sorrow over his lost love, Lenore. This is happening at midnight, in December. Perhaps it is New Year's Eve, since the narrator says, "Eagerly I wished the morrow" because he wants to make a fresh start. The reading wasn't helping to ease his sorrow, so he was nearly asleep. As this is happening, the narrator hears a knocking at his door.

Below are the next two stanzas of "The Raven."

Stanza 3

And the silken sad uncertain rustling of each purple curtain

Thrilled me - filled me with fantastic terrors never felt before;

So that now, to still the beating of my heart, I stood repeating

`'Tis some visitor entreating entrance at my chamber door -

Some late visitor entreating entrance at my chamber door; -

This it is, and nothing more,'

Stanza 4

Presently my heart grew stronger; hesitating then no longer,

`Sir,' said I, `or Madam, truly your forgiveness I implore;

But the fact is I was napping, and so gently you came rapping,

And so faintly you came tapping, tapping at my chamber door,

That I scarce was sure I heard you' - here I opened wide the door; -

Darkness there, and nothing more.

Remember, in order to understand poems, you usually have to read them more carefully than other types of writing. Here are some things you need to do to understand a poem:

1. Make sure you know what all the words mean.

    In the stanzas above, "entreating" means "an earnest request."

    "Implore" means "to beg for, urgently."

2. Look carefully at word order.

    Instead of saying, "hesitating then no longer," we would normally say, "no longer hesitating."

3. Look for hints about the setting of the poem.

4. Look for figurative language.

Part B - Poetry

Directions: Answer the questions about the section of "The Raven" presented in Part A.

1. The dark mood of the poem continues in these stanzas. List at least two words or phrases that contribute to that mood.

2. In stanza 3, the narrator is afraid. He tries to convince himself of what?

_____

3. How do we know the narrator is afraid?

_____

4. In stanza 4, the narrator is apologizing to the person at the door. Why?

_____

5. What does he see when he finally opens the door?

_____

Part C- Summarize Passage

Directions: Read the passage and then follow the directions.

The United States developed into a powerful industrial nation after the Civil War. There were, however, many problems that came with the changing American way of life. Many immigrants and farmers were heading to the cities for jobs, the South could no longer rely upon slavery, and cities were growing not only in population, but also in the number of factories they had. Not everyone living in cities lived in ideal conditions. Former slaves from the South definitely did not. Many were denied the freedoms and rights that other citizens enjoyed. People working to improve these conditions in America were called "reformers." Dorothea Dix and Horace Mann were among the reformers working before the American Civil War. As time progressed, new reformers stepped forward and worked to improve the lives of the urban poor, African-Americans, women, and farmers.

Write a summary list for this passage. Note that some ideas have been listed for you.

Summary List:

1. After the American Civil War, the United States was a strong industrial nation.

2. Life was changing as cities were becoming crowded with immigrants, those leaving farms, freed slaves from the South, and workers arriving to work in the newly built factories

_____

_____

Finally, use the list to help you write a short summary of the passage, in your own words.
A summary should be two or three sentences long.

_____

_____

_____

_____

Part D - Main Idea

Directions: Below is the main idea statement for the passage in Part C. Write a detail from the passage that supports the main idea statement.

Reformers worked to improve the living conditions of many people caught up in the rapid growth and change in the United States during the Industrial Age.

_____

_____

_____

Part E - Review

Directions: Read the passage and then answer the questions.

Have you ever heard of a man named Lewis Latimer? You may never have heard his name, but every day you probably use what he helped to invent. Lewis Latimer was instrumental in the invention of both the light bulb and the telephone.

Lewis Latimer, an African American, was born in Massachusetts in 1848. Just six years before his birth, his parents had escaped slavery in Virginia and had moved north. Lewis was an excellent student who loved drawing and reading. However, it was very difficult for his family to earn a living during those times so he spent most of his time working with his father at various odd jobs.

With the blight of slavery ongoing and the Civil War raging, Lewis joined the Navy in 1864 to help support his family. He was only 16 years old at the time and had to lie about his age in order to join.

After the war there were many new inventions on the market. The government created a special protection for new and useful inventions called a patent. Once an inventor is granted a patent no one may use, make or sell the invention without the inventor's permission. When Latimer got out of the Navy, he went to work as an office boy for a Boston firm that helped inventors file for and get patents. While working there he found he had a talent for mechanical drawing. Latimer watched the skilled draftsmen who worked at the firm. He read every book on mechanical drawing that he could get his hands on. He taught himself how to use the tools of the trade. When he was given the opportunity to show the firm's owners what he could do, they promoted him to draftsman.

While working at the Boston firm, Lewis met an inventor named Alexander Graham Bell who needed a draftsman to help him draw blueprints for a new invention . . . the telephone. Bell hired Lewis to be his draftsman, and working together almost around the clock they finished the plans. In 1876 they were the first people to file for a patent for the telephone. In 1880 Latimer went to work for the US Electric Lighting Company and invented a new carbon filament for the light bulb. In 1884 he was hired by another famous inventor, Thomas Edison, to work at the Edison Company. Latimer's expertise as a draftsman and electrical engineer were instrumental in helping Thomas Edison get countless patents. Lewis Latimer had the distinction of being the only African American member of the *Edison Pioneers*, the engineering division of the Edison Company.

1. Which of the following sentences expresses the author's specific purpose?

    a. The author's purpose is to persuade the reader to become an inventor.

    b. The author's purpose is to inform the reader about the life and work of Lewis Latimer.

    c. The author's purpose is to inform the reader about how to draw blueprints.

    d. The author's purpose is to inform the reader about patents.

2. In the passage, the words *had the distinction* as well as *being the only* are used to inform the reader that:

    a. It was very easy to become a member of the Edison Pioneers.

    b. It was a rare honor to be a member of the Edison Pioneers and no other African American had achieved that level of success.

    c. People got discouraged if they weren't made members of the Edison Pioneers.

    d. The engineering division of the Edison Company was unique.

3. Which of the following is a fact stated in the passage?

    a. Latimer was 16 when he joined the Navy.

    b. Most inventions are not granted a patent.

    c. A patent is a special legal protection for a new invention.

    d. If you get a patent, you'll become rich.

4. Which of the following characteristics would probably ***not*** apply to an inventor?

    a. clever

    b. fearful

    c. adventurous

    d. smart

5. Which of these questions does the second paragraph answer?

    a. When did Latimer go to work for Thomas Edison?

    b. In what state was Lewis Latimer born?

    c. What branch of the military did Lewis join?

    d. Where was Latimer working when he met Alexander Graham Bell?

Part F - Bonus

Look at the line below from "The Raven."

And´ so | faint´ly | you´ came | tap´ping, | tap´ping | at´ my | cham´ber | door´,

This line is made up of eight **trochaic** metrical feet, or groups of syllables with one accented syllable, followed by one unaccented syllable. Notice that the last "foot" is a short one. It has just one accented syllable that isn't followed by an unaccented syllable.

Trochee and **trochaic** come from a Greek word that means "run."

BONUS REVIEW

The **rhyming pattern** of a stanza uses letters to show which words at the ends of lines rhyme.

Here is a familiar verse:

Roses are red, violets are blue,

Sugar is sweet, and so are you.

The **rhyming pattern** of these two lines is: a a.

Lesson 33

Part A - Poetry

In the third and fourth stanzas of Poe's "The Raven," the narrator is afraid because of the knocking at his door. He tries to convince himself that it's just a late visitor by repeating to himself, "...visitor entreating entrance at my chamber door." He then works up his courage and apologizes to whoever is at the door, saying he had almost been asleep, and wasn't sure he'd heard the knocking. When he opened his door to greet his visitor, no one was there.

Below are the next two stanzas of "The Raven."

<u>Stanza 5</u>

Deep into that darkness peering, long I stood there wondering, fearing,

Doubting, dreaming dreams no mortal ever dared to dream to dream before

But the silence was unbroken, and the darkness gave no token,

And the only word there spoken was the whispered word, `Lenore!'

This I whispered, and an echo murmured back the word, `Lenore!'

Merely this and nothing more.

<u>Stanza 6</u>

Back into the chamber turning, all my soul within me burning,

Soon again I heard a tapping somewhat louder than before.

`Surely,' said I, `surely that is something at my window lattice;

Let me see then, what the threat is, and this mystery explore -

Let my heart be still a moment and this mystery explore; -

'Tis the wind and nothing more!'

Note:

1. "Token" means "a sign."

2. A "lattice" is a decoration made of strips of wood that criss-cross one another.

Part B - Poetry

Directions: Answer the questions about the section of "The Raven" presented in Part A.

1. Rewrite the first line in stanza 5, using conventional word order.

_____

_____

2. The narrator is depressed over having lost Lenore, who has died. What does he mean when he says, "dreaming dreams no mortal ever dared to dream to dream before?"

_____

_____

3. The narrator whispers Lenore's name. Then what happens?

_____

_____

4.   Knowing there is no one at the door, the narrator decides the tapping sound is coming from where?

_____

_____

5.   The words, "let my heart be still," indicate that the narrator is feeling:

   a.   content

   b.   afraid

   c.   confident

   d.   tired

Part C- Summarize Passage

Directions: Read the passage, and then follow the directions.

In the early 1900's, Americans were beginning to read stories about dishonest practices in business and government. The suffering of poor people in big cities was brought into their homes by way of newspaper and magazine articles.

Muckrakers were a group of writers in the early 1900's who exposed social and political wrongs in the United States. In 1906, President Theodore Roosevelt labeled them "muckrakers" because he felt they only wrote about the unpleasant, dirty side of American life. But, these writers made the public aware of social problems and forced the government and businesses to work to solve them.

The muckrakers helped pave the way for many reforms in the United States. When readers could actually see pictures of the living conditions that were described in the articles, they began to take action. Many joined the demand for better housing, better living and working conditions, and decent schools. For example, Upton Sinclair's novel, *The Jungle*, exposed unsanitary conditions in the meat-packing industry. This exposure led to the nation's first pure food laws.

Write a summary list for this passage. Note that some ideas have been listed for you.

Summary List:

1. In the early 1900's, the American people were made aware of problems in government and society by reading magazine and newspaper articles.

2. Muckrakers were journalists who discovered wrong-doings in society and wrote about them.

_____

_____

Finally, use the list to help you write a short summary of the passage, in your own words.

A summary should be two or three sentences long.

_____

_____

_____

_____

Part D - Main Idea

Directions: Below is the main idea statement for the passage in Part C. Write a detail from the passage that supports the main idea statement.

Muckrakers were responsible for many reforms by informing the public of wrong doings in business and society.

_____

_____

_____

Part E - Review

Directions: Refer to the passage in Part C to answer the following questions.

1. Which of the following sentences expresses the author's specific purpose?

   a. The author's purpose is to persuade the reader that President Roosevelt was wrong about the muckrakers.

   b. The author's purpose is to inform the reader about why the muckrakers took the action they took, and the effect their work had on society.

   c. The author's purpose is to inform the reader about all the things that were being hidden from the American people before the work of the muckrakers.

   d. The author's purpose is to entertain the reader with a story about the life of a muckraker.

2. Which of the following words would best describe the work of the muckrakers?

   a. honest

   b. scary

   c. selfish

   d. mean-spirited

3. If you were reporting on something you discovered that was harmful to people, which of the following would probably be a good idea?

   a. getting the permission of whomever you were reporting on before the article was printed

   b. making sure you put your opinion into the article

   c. making sure your had all the facts before printing the article

   d. making sure no one else had reported on the same thing

4. Choose the best possible meaning for the underlined word in the model sentence.

   Model: Muckrakers were a group of writers in the early 1900's who <u>exposed</u> social and political wrongs in the United States.

   a. passed laws against

   b. ignored

   c. took part in

   d. uncovered

5. The article doesn't tell you exactly, but what might the muckrakers find to write about in the lives of an immigrant, a freed slave living in the North, or a farmer now living in the city?

_____

_____

_____

6. Choose the best possible meaning for the underlined word in the model sentence.

   Model: Outstanding muckrakers, such as Ida M. Tarbell, exposed the corruption in the Standard Oil Company, and it's <u>monopoly</u> of the oil industry.

   a. a popular family board game

   b. total control

   c. ownership

   d. expansion

7. According to the article, all of the following can be associated with muckrakers except:

   a. *The Jungle*

   b. President Theodore Roosevelt

   c. newspapers and magazines

   d. radio

Part F - Bonus

Each of the following words could be a **trochaic foot** in a poem:

   pat´tern   hill´side   mus´tang   bed´time   wal´let

Each word has two syllables. The first syllable in each word is accented, and the second is unaccented.
If you say words like this loudly, the accented syllable stands out clearly.

BONUS REVIEW

A **cognitive map** is a representation of someone's thinking. Here is a simple **cognitive map**:

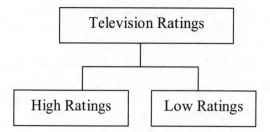

The word **cognitive** comes from the Greek word *gno*, which means "to know."

Lesson 34

Part A - Poetry

In the fifth and sixth stanzas of Poe's "The Raven," the narrator sees no one when he opens his door, and dares to hope that Lenore has returned from the dead. But when he says her name, all he hears is the name echoing back to him. He decides the tapping noise must be caused by the wind blowing against a lattice around the outside of his window. He tries to calm himself in order to check out the window.

Below are the next two stanzas of "The Raven."

Stanza 7

Open here I flung the shutter, when, with many a flirt and flutter,

In there stepped a stately raven of the saintly days of yore.

Not the least obeisance made he; not an instant stopped or stayed he;

But, with mien of lord or lady, perched above my chamber door -

Perched upon a bust of Pallas just above my chamber door -

Perched, and sat, and nothing more.

Stanza 8

Then this ebony bird beguiling my sad fancy into smiling,

By the grave and stern decorum of the countenance it wore,

`Though thy crest be shorn and shaven, thou,' I said, `art sure no craven.

Ghastly grim and ancient raven wandering from the nightly shore -

Tell me what thy lordly name is on the Night's Plutonian shore!'

Quoth the raven, `Nevermore.'

Note:

1. "Obeisance" is related to the word obey. It is an attitude of respect.
2. "Mien" means "the attitude a person shows."
3. "Pallas" was the goddess of wisdom in Greek mythology.
4. "Beguile" means "to distract."
5. "Craven," used as a noun, means "a coward."
6. "Pluto" was the god of the underworld in Roman mythology.

Part B - Poetry

Directions: Answer the questions about the section of "The Raven" presented in Part A.

1. What happened when the narrator opened his shutters?

2. Most of stanza 7 describes the raven. How does the raven act?
    a. frightened
    b. upset
    c. naughty
    d. confident

3. The raven perches on a statue of Pallas, the goddess of wisdom. What might that tell us about the narrator?

4. What question does the narrator ask the raven near the end of stanza 8?

5. What answer does the raven give?

6. Which two words rhyme in the first line of stanza 7?

Part C- Summarize Passage

Directions: Read the passage, and then follow the directions.

People who stayed on farms in the late 1800's and early 1900's were as unhappy as poor workers in the cities. New farm machinery of the time made it possible for farmers to grow more crops for market than ever before. Instead of making more money, however, they found the demand for their products was far less than the supply. The high rates that were charged by railroads to transport their crops to market angered farmers, too.

The farmers banded together for more power and a bigger say in the government. They formed their own organizations known as the "People's Party" or "Populist Party." The Populist Party nominated its own presidential candidate, William Jennings Bryan, for the 1892 election. In the end, another candidate backed by big business won the election. That marked the end of the Populists as a political party.

Write a summary list for this passage. Note that some ideas have been listed for you.

Summary List:
1. New machinery made it possible for farmers to produce bigger crops.
2. Farmers were often poor because of high prices for shipping and a low demand for crops.

_____

_____

Finally, use the list to help you write a short summary of the passage, in your own words. A summary should be two or three sentences long.

_____

_____

_____

_____

Part D - Main Idea

Directions: Below is the main idea statement for the passage in Part C. Write TWO details from the passage that support the main idea statement.

In the late 1800s and early 1900s, American farmers, angered over decreased demand and increased shipping prices for their crops, created their own political party known as the Populist Party.

_____

_____

_____

_____

Part E - Review

Directions: Read the passage and then answer the question.

After the Civil War, African-Americans were no longer slaves, and were entitled to the opportunities that the American way of life offered. This was not always a reality, however. As slaves, many blacks were unable to attend school. Booker T. Washington believed that education was the way for black people to have a better life, and he devoted his life to making that possible. As president of the Tuskegee Institute in Alabama, a school for black people, he was one of the most famous African-American leaders and educators of his day. The Tuskegee Institute prepared black people to become teachers and skilled tradesmen. George Washington Carver joined the faculty and taught modern farming techniques. Washington believed that black people should develop skills that would help them make a living. He thought that they would eventually win equality with whites by being patient and working hard.

All African-Americans, however, did not agree with Washington's views on winning equality. W. E. B. Du Bois was one of the most powerful African-American leaders of the twentieth century. He urged blacks to take pride in their culture and to aggressively, not quietly, protest discrimination. He did not agree with Booker T. Washington's ideas that education and patience would be enough to gradually integrate African-Americans into white society. Instead,

Du Bois demanded immediate equal rights for African-Americans in politics and society. Together with other well-educated black and white reformers, he helped form the National Association for the Advancement of Colored People. This organization is more commonly known as the NAACP. Du Bois frequently clashed with other African-American leaders who supported a more gradual method of integration. The NAACP is still a leading organization in the fight for racial equality. Eventually, W. E. B. Du Bois moved to Africa, and he gave up his American citizenship shortly before his death in 1963.

1. Which of the following sentences expresses the author's specific purpose?

   a. The author's purpose is to persuade the reader that African-Americans needed to be educated in order to gain equal rights.

   b. The author's purpose is to inform the reader about the Tuskegee Institute.

   c. The author's purpose is to explain to the reader the different approaches to gaining racial equality used by two powerful African-American leaders.

   d. The author's purpose is to persuade the reader that the only way African-Americans could integrate into white society was by fighting for their rights.

2. The story doesn't tell you, but which character trait best describes W. E. B. Du Bois?

   a. reckless

   b. determined

   c. mild mannered

   d. patient

3. Which statement best summarizes the passage?

   a. Two powerful leaders dealt with the problem of gaining equal rights for African-Americans in different ways.

   b. A powerful black leader moved to Africa and gave up his American citizenship.

   c. A college for black people was started in Alabama in the hopes that education would lead to integration and equal rights.

   d. An organization begun many years ago for the purpose of fighting for racial equality is still strong today.

4. What did the addition of George Washington Carver bring to the Tuskegee Institute?

   a. Many new books were donated to the library.

   b. A sports program was added.

   c. Classes were taught for those wanting to become teachers.

   d. The teaching of modern farming methods was added.

5. All of the following names are mentioned in the passage *except*:

    a. W. E. B. Du Bois

    b. George Washington Carver

    c. Ida B. Wells

    d. Booker T. Washington

Follow the instructions using information from the passage and the diagram below.

6. Which of the following would make a good title for the diagram below?

    a. The Lives of Two Famous African-Americans

    b. African-American Reformers

    c. Two Paths to Equality

    d. Education is a Way to Equality

7. Circle the part of the passage that would go in Booker T. Washington's **belief** circle.

8. Circle the part of the passage that would go in W. E. B. Du Bois's **belief** circle.

9. What information from the passage should be put by the second dot in the Tuskegee Institute box?

10. The passage doesn't tell you, but learning to become a skilled tradesman would include all of the following occupations *except*:

    a. blacksmith

    b. carpenter

    c. traveling salesman

    d. silversmith

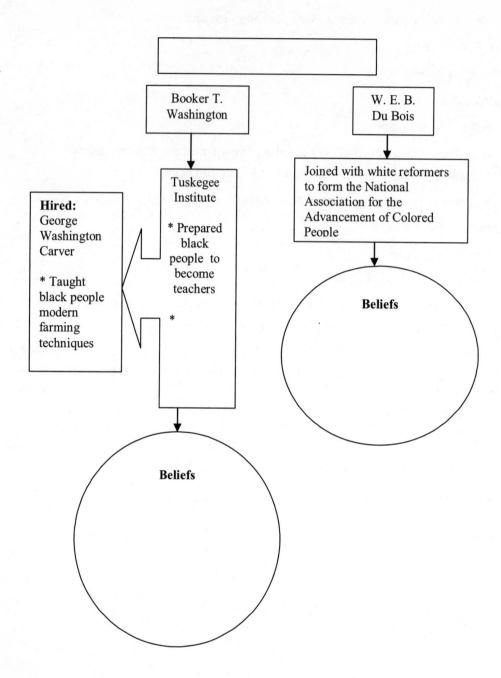

Part F - Bonus

Look at the line below from "The Raven."

> But´ the | si´lence | was´ un | bro´ken, | and´ the | dark´ness | gave´ no | to´ken,

This line is made up of eight **trochaic** metrical feet which are groups of syllables with one accented syllable, followed by one unaccented syllable.

Trochee and **trochaic** come from a Greek word that means "run."

Lesson 36

Part A - Poetry

In the seventh and eighth stanzas of Poe's "The Raven," the narrator opens his window shutters and a raven flies into the house. The raven acts as if it belongs in the narrator's room. The raven just sits silently on a perch above the narrator's door, until the narrator asks the bird it's name. The raven answers, "Nevermore."

Below are the next two stanzas of "The Raven."

<u>Stanza 9</u>

Much I marveled this ungainly fowl to hear discourse so plainly,

Though its answer little meaning - little relevancy bore;

For we cannot help agreeing that no living human being

Ever yet was blessed with seeing bird above his chamber door -

Bird or beast above the sculptured bust above his chamber door,

With such name as `Nevermore.'

<u>Stanza 10</u>

But the raven, sitting lonely on the placid bust, spoke only,

That one word, as if his soul in that one word he did outpour.

Nothing further then he uttered - not a feather then he fluttered -

Till I scarcely more than muttered `Other friends have flown before -

On the morrow will he leave me, as my hopes have flown before.'

Then the bird said, `Nevermore.'

Note:

1. "Discourse" means "something said," in either speech or writing.

2. In the third line of Stanza 9, the word "for" means "because."

3. The rhyming pattern of each stanza is the same. We can use letters to show which words at the ends of the lines rhyme with which other words. Here is the pattern for Stanza 9:

a plainly

b bore

c being

b door

b door

b nevermore

Part B - Poetry

Directions: Answer the questions about the section of "The Raven" in Part A.

1. Paraphrase the first line of Stanza 9.

_____

_____

2. What do lines 3 and 4 of stanza 9 mean?

_____

_____

3. What does the raven do up until the narrator mutters something?

_____

4. Who is the narrator talking about when he says, "Other friends have flown before-"?

_____

5. Talking to himself out loud, the narrator asks himself if the raven will leave the next day. What does the raven say?

_____

Part C - Summarize Passages

Directions: Read the passage and then follow the directions.

Geographers look closely at why people choose to live in a certain place. Did the natural resources of the area have anything to do with why they chose one place over another? It certainly did when people began to settle in America. They looked for places that had enough natural resources to provide them with food, water, clothing, and shelter.

Once settled, people begin to shape their environment constantly. Farmers used the soil for growing crops or grazing animals. They used ponds for water. They cut trees to build fences to keep their animals from running away. In cities, people cut into hillsides or cut down wooded areas to build houses, businesses, or shopping malls.

The environment can also shape people. For example, roads sometimes have to be built around mountains, and bridges need to be built over rivers. Storm walls need to be built to keep the ocean from washing over the beaches. Some homes built on the coast are built on stilts for protection from storm tides or floods.

Write a summary list for this passage. Note that some have been listed for you.

Summary List:
1. Natural resources influenced places where early American pioneers settled.
2. People shape and change their environment.

_____

Finally, use the list to help you write a short summary of the passage, in your own words.
A summary should be two or three sentences long.

_____

_____

_____

Part D - Main Idea

Directions: In the statements below, an _X_ is placed next to three details from the passage in Part C. The letters _TG_ are placed next to the statement that is too general to be a good title for the passage. Beside the letters _MI_, write a main idea statement for the passage.

_X_ Natural resources help people decide where they want to live.

_X_ Geographers look closely at how locations on the earth can be compared.

_TG_ Geography: The Study of Earth and Its Inhabitants

_X_ People are constantly changing the environment.

_MI_

Part E - Review

Directions: Read the following passage and then answer the questions.

It's shiny, it's safe, and it can hold things together, as well as being multi-useful. How many times have you heard someone ask the question, "Does anyone have a _____? It's an emergency! The words most likely used to fill in the bank are "safety pin."

The safety pin is the invention of a mechanic from New York named Walter Hunt. Walter Hunt also built America's first sewing machine. He later lost interest in patenting his sewing machine because he believed the invention would cause a rise in unemployment. The safety pin was invented while Walter Hunt was twisting a piece of wire, trying to think of something that would help him pay off a fifteen dollar debt. On April 10, 1849, the safety pin was patented. Walter Hunt didn't think much of his safety pin as an invention, so he soon sold the patent for four hundred dollars. Then, he watched as the buyer proceeded to become a millionaire!

1. Which of the following sentences expresses the author's specific purpose.

    a. The author's purpose is to persuade the reader that the safety pin is a very important invention.

    b. The author's purpose is to explain to the reader why Walter Hunt invented the safety pin.

    c. The author's purpose is to inform the reader about the life of Walter Hunt.

    d. The author's purpose is to inform the reader about the inventor, and the event, that lead to the invention of the safety pin.

2. Which characteristic would probably best describe Walter Hunt?

    a. adventurous

    b. guilty

    c. competitive

    d. easy going

3. Which one of the following idioms would best apply to this passage?

    a. Necessity is the mother of invention.

    b. Nothing will come of nothing.

    c. bee in your bonnet

    d. bite the dust

4. Based on the information in the passage about Walter Hunt, what would probably happen if he invented something else?

    _____

    _____

5. Walter Hunt was trying to think of something useful to do with a piece of wire in order to pay off a:

    a. debate

    b. debt

    c. deal

    d. debit

Part F - Bonus

You know that **rhyming** words end with exactly the same sounds: rang and sang, for example.

Many times, poets use **partial rhymes**. Words that end with similar sounds—but not exactly the same—are **partial rhymes**. There are several names for **partial rhymes** that you don't have to remember: slant rhymes, oblique rhymes, half rhymes, and near rhymes.

Here are some examples of **partial rhymes**: dry and die; moon and grown; rang and rag.

Lesson 37

Part A - Poetry

In the ninth and tenth stanzas of Poe's "The Raven," the narrator expresses surprise that the bird spoke to him so clearly. The narrator is also surprised that a bird, or any animal, is perched on a statue above his door. The narrator tells us that other than saying "Nevermore" after being asked its name, the raven doesn't do anything at all: doesn't speak again, doesn't move a feather. Then, mumbling to himself out loud, the narrator wonders if the raven will be gone the next day, just as Lenore left him. Although the narrator was not speaking to the raven, the raven says, "Nevermore."

Below are the next two stanzas of "The Raven."

<u>Stanza 11</u>

Startled at the stillness broken by reply so aptly spoken,

`Doubtless,' said I, `what it utters is its only stock and store,

Caught from some unhappy master whom unmerciful disaster

Followed fast and followed faster till his songs one burden bore -

Till the dirges of his hope that melancholy burden bore

Of "Never-nevermore.'"

<u>Stanza 12</u>

But the raven still beguiling all my sad soul into smiling,

Straight I wheeled a cushioned seat in front of bird and bust and door;

Then, upon the velvet sinking, I betook myself to linking

Fancy unto fancy, thinking what this ominous bird of yore -

What this grim, ungainly, gaunt, and ominous bird of yore

Meant in croaking `Nevermore.'

Note:
1. "Stock and store" means "acquired."
2. "Dirge" means "a funeral hymn," or some other slow, sad song.
3. "Melancholy" means "sad," "depressed," or "gloomy."
4. An old meaning of the word "betake" is "commit." The past tense form of betake is betook (just like take and took).

5. "Ominous" means "threatening."

Part B - Poetry

Directions: Answer the questions about the section of "The Raven" in Part A.

1. What does "caught from some unhappy master" probably mean?

_____

_____

2. The narrator speculates that the raven's owner repeated the word "Nevermore" over and over again, many times. Why would he make that guess?

_____

_____

3. Why does the narrator think the bird's master was unhappy?

_____

_____

4. In Stanza 12, the narrator is still fascinated by the raven. Here, though, he begins to think the raven has NOT just memorized the word nevermore. Which words tell us that?

_____

_____

Part C- Summarize Passage

Directions: Read the passage and then follow the directions.

At one time or another, each one of us has picked up a rock. There may have been something special about that rock that caught our eye. Maybe it sparkled, maybe it was made of many different colors, or maybe it had an odd shape to it. Maybe it contained the fossil remains of ancient plants or animals.

Geologists collect and study rocks. Geologists are able to "read" the earth's history by closely studying the rocks and the formations they came from. To geologists, rocks and minerals can tell the journey the earth took from the past to the present. They may also be able to tell what the earth might be like millions of years from now.

Write a summary list for this passage.

Summary List:

_____

_____

_____

Finally, use the list to help you write a short summary of the passage, in your own words. A summary should be two or three sentences long.

_____

_____

_____

_____

Part D - Main Idea

Directions: In the statements below, an *X* is placed next to three details from the passage in Part C. The letters *TG* are placed next to the statement that would be too general to be a main idea statement. Beside the letters *MI*, write a main idea statement for the passage.

X Geologists collect and study rocks.

X People are attracted to rocks because they may be pretty or odd shaped.

TG Rocks are full of information.

X Rocks may contain fossils of ancient plants and animals.

MI _____

_____

Part E - Review

Directions: Read the passage and then answer the questions.

Waterfalls come in many shapes and sizes. Some are tall and narrow, while others can be many miles wide. Smaller waterfalls that carry a small volume of water are called cascades. Falls with a large volume of water are referred to as cataracts.

Rapids and waterfalls are the result of water wearing down layers of soft rock in a stream or river bed. This erosion of soft rock sometimes develops into a cliff. When the river flows over the cliff, it creates a waterfall.

Niagara Falls is one of the world's most famous waterfalls. The Falls is located on the Niagara River between Lake Erie and Lake Ontario. Niagara Falls is really formed from two waterfalls; Horseshoe Falls is in Ontario, Canada, and American Falls is in New York. Most of the water at Niagara Falls flows over the Horseshoe Falls.

The Falls is continuously being eroded by the force of water wearing away the soft rock. Horseshoe Falls wears away at a rate of 3 inches to 6 feet per year. American Falls erodes more slowly because less water flows over it. About 1 inch wears away from American Falls each year. It is estimated that Niagara Falls has moved back 7 miles from where it first began.

Niagara Falls was probably formed about 12,000 years ago, after the last great ice sheet melted from the region. The melting ice caused Lake Erie to overflow. The overflow formed the Niagara River. The river ran northward over a high cliff. The Niagara River cut through the escarpment, and over the centuries Niagara Falls was formed.

In the past, waterfalls were used to turn water wheels. Water wheels changed the energy of falling water into mechanical energy that could be used for running machinery. The earliest water wheels were used mainly to grind grain. Water wheels were a major source of power until the development of the steam engine. Today many waterfalls are used to generate hydroelectric power.

1. Which of the following sentences expresses the author's specific purpose?

    a. The author's purpose is to persuade the reader to experience the beauty and power of a waterfall by making a visit to one, and learning its history.

    b. The author's purpose is to explain to the reader how waterfalls form.

    c. The author's purpose is to inform the reader about the formation and uses of waterfalls in general, using Niagara Falls as an example.

    d. The author's purpose is to entertain the reader with a story about visiting Niagara Falls.

2. Which of the following statements is an *opinion*?

    a. Niagara Falls is shared by both Canada and the United States.

    b. Niagara Falls is a cataract.

    c. Niagara Falls would be a great place for a family vacation.

    d. More Americans than Canadians visit Niagara Falls.

3. Choose the best possible meaning for the underlined word in the model sentence.
    Model: The Niagara River cut through the <u>escarpment</u>, and over the centuries, Niagara Falls was formed.

    a. steep cliff

    b. riverbed

    c. dam

    d. lake

4. Water has been used for each of the following kinds of power **except. (Note:** there are TWO correct answers)

    a. nuclear

    b. electrical

    c. mechanical

    d. radiant

Use the chart below to answer questions # 5 and # 6.

5. According to the chart, which waterfall is the highest?

    a. Tugela

    b. Angel

    c. Tyssestrengene

    d. Yosemite

6. Which waterfall is almost exactly 1000 feet higher than L. Mar Valley?

    a. Yosemite

    b. Utigord

    c. Tugela

    d. Monge

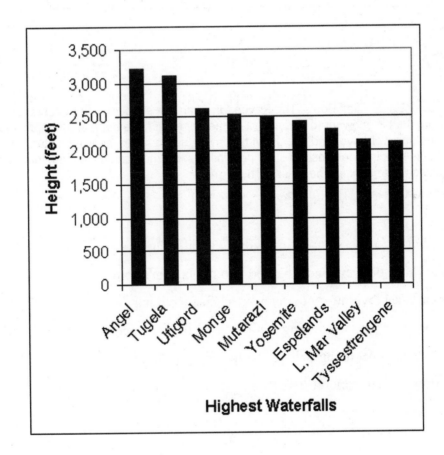

Part F - Bonus

Here are some **partial rhymes**, words that end with similar sounds, but not exactly the same sounds:

play and plate   hour and corner   evil and devil   actor and fiber

BONUS REVIEW

An example of an **idiom** is "pull the wool over someone's eyes."

This is an old **idiom** in American English. Back when men wore powdered wigs made from wool, someone would be temporarily unable to see if you pulled their wig down over their eyes.

The meaning of the **idiom** is "to deceive someone."

Lesson 38

Part A - Poetry

In the eleventh stanza of Edgar Allen Poe's "The Raven," the narrator speculates that the raven learned to say the word "nevermore" from the bird's owner (or master). The master must have been an unhappy person, the narrator believes, who repeated the word over and over, until the raven learned it. In the twelfth stanza, however, the narrator begins to let his imagination consider other possibilities. He then begins to think that maybe the raven is trying to communicate some meaning when it says "nevermore."

Below are the next two stanzas of "The Raven."

Stanza 13

This I sat engaged in guessing, but no syllable expressing

To the fowl whose fiery eyes now burned into my bosom's core;

This and more I sat divining, with my head at ease reclining

On the cushion's velvet violet lining that the lamp-light gloated o'er,

But whose velvet violet lining with the lamp-light gloating o'er,

She shall press, ah, nevermore!

Stanza 14

Then, methought, the air grew denser, perfumed from an unseen censer

Swung by angels whose faint foot-falls tinkled on the tufted floor.

`Wretch,' I cried, `thy God hath lent thee - by these angels he has sent thee

Respite - respite and nepenthe from the memories of Lenore!

Quaff, oh quaff this kind nepenthe, and forget this lost Lenore!'

Quoth the raven, `Nevermore.'

Note:

1. To "divine" something means "to see into the future."

2. A "censer" is a type of container used to burn incense.

3. "Respite" means "a brief rest."

4. In ancient Greece, "Nepenthe" was thought to be a drug that relieved grief.

Part B - Poetry

Directions: Answer the questions about the section of "The Raven" in Part A.

1. The first word in Stanza 13, "this," refers back to Stanza 12, where the narrator wonders what the raven means when it says "nevermore." The narrator is thinking about that in the beginning of Stanza 13 when he says, "but no syllable expressing To the fowl." What does that mean?

_____

_____

2. In Stanza 12, the narrator "wheeled a cushioned seat in front of bird." Describe the chair. Look back to Stanza 12 if you need to.

_____

_____

3. The light of the lamp "gloats" over the chair. This is figurative language. Gloating is feeling great pleasure, usually from something unpleasant that happened to someone else. How might the light gloat over the velvet violet lining of the chair?

   a. The light shows the color of the chair.

   b. The light is happy that the raven is in the room.

   c. The narrator thinks the light feels pleasure over Lenore being gone and the narrator being miserable.

4. What does this line mean: "She shall press, ah, nevermore!"

_____

_____

5. In Stanza 14, the narrator cries out that God has sent the raven to give him some brief relief from his grief over Lenore. Why might we think the narrator won't really get that relief?

_____

_____

Part C- Summarize Passage

Directions: Read the passage and then follow the directions.

"Rain, rain go away; come again some other day." We mutter that phrase whenever we wish it would stop raining. Most of the time, the rain does go away once it strikes the ground.

Each raindrop is actually like a tiny hammer, hitting the ground hard enough to wear away the surface. It sometimes strikes with enough force to break tiny pieces from solid rock. Often, water and undissolved particles clog the pores of the ground and prevent rainwater from sinking in. What is the result? Puddles!

If there is too much rain, it begins to collect and flow over the ground. This water is called *runoff*. If it rains really hard, most of the rainwater becomes runoff. This runoff quickly collects soil and rocks as it flows along, scraping the ground like a fingernail file.

The runoff carries its load to the nearest stream, causing it to swell. Now the swollen stream scrapes away the land as it flows to the nearest river. You can guess what happens next. The swollen river flows toward the sea, continuing the scraping, only on a much larger scale, until it reaches the sea, where it dumps all its contents.

Write a summary list for this passage.

Summary List:

_____

_____

_____

_____

Finally, use the list to help you write a short summary of the passage, in your own words.
A summary should be two or three sentences long.

_____

_____

_____

_____

Part D - Main Idea

Directions: In the statements below, an *X* is placed next to three details from the passage in Part C. The letters *TG* are placed next to the statement that would be too general to be a main idea statement. Beside the letters *MI*, write a main idea statement for the passage.

    TG Water is very powerful.

    X Falling raindrops can break off small pieces of rock.

    X Puddles form when rain doesn't soak into the ground.

    X Too much rain becomes runoff.

MI

_____

_____

Part E - Review

Directions: Re-read the passage in Part C and then answer the questions.

1. Which of the following would be most like the situation in the model sentence?

    Model: Water and undissolved particles clog the pores of the ground and prevent rainwater from sinking in.

    a. Draining the water from the pan after cooking spaghetti.

    b. Water collecting in the shower because the drain is stopped up.

    c. Rinsing the shampoo out of your hair in the shower.

    d. Using a sponge to wipe up spilled water.

2. Which of the following words could best be substituted in the passage for "fingernail file"?

    a. saw

    b. toothbrush

    c. sandpaper

    d. rake

3. Look at the underlined word in the model sentence. Then choose the sentence that uses the underlined word in the same way as the model sentence.

    Model: As raindrops strike the soil, they make tiny craters.

    a. Last night I had so much trouble getting to sleep I heard the clock strike midnight.

    b. After months of trying to reach a settlement, the workers finally voted to go on strike.

    c. If you can strike the match, I'll hold the candle next to the flame.

    d. The waves will soon begin to strike the shore as the storm grows stronger.

4. Using information from the passage, place the following events in the correct order by placing the letter and the accompanying text in the appropriate box of the chart below. Some of the boxes have been filled in for you.

    a. Puddles form.

    b. Swollen streams collect more soil and flow into rivers.

    c. Rivers carry deposits from streams and collect more soil on their way to the sea.

    d. Runoff water collects soil and pieces of rock.

    e. Raindrops fall.

    f. Rivers dump their contents into the sea.

    g. Ground pores get clogged.

    h. Soil and rock are pounded.

    i. Runoff flows into swollen streams.

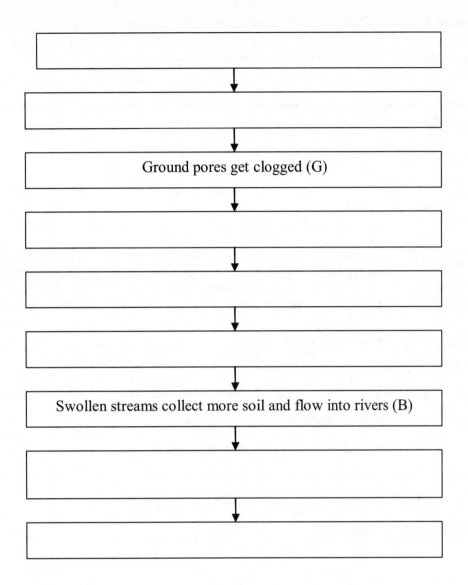

Ground pores get clogged (G)

Swollen streams collect more soil and flow into rivers (B)

Part F - Bonus

Here are two lists, one of words that **rhyme**, and one of **partial rhymes**.

Rhyming Words	**Partial Rhymes**
admit and commit	commit and comment
that and combat	that and than
court and sport	sport and part

BONUS REVIEW

Look at the line below from "The Raven."

De´so | la´te yet | all´ un | daunt´ed, | on´ this | des´ert | land´ en | chant´ed

This line is made up of eight **trochaic** metrical feet: groups of syllables with one accented syllable, followed by one unaccented syllable.

Trochee and **trochaic** come from a Greek word that means "run."

Lesson 39

Part A - Poetry

In the thirteenth stanza of Poe's "The Raven," the narrator is thinking about what the raven might mean by saying "nevermore." The narrator is sitting in his comfortable, violet velvet chair, thinking that Lenore will never sit in that chair again. In Stanza 14, the narrator tries to convince himself that perhaps the raven is there to give him some relief from the loss of Lenore, but the raven says "nevermore" again, suggesting that there is no relief from the narrator's grief.

Below are the next two stanzas of "The Raven."

<u>Stanza 15</u>

`Prophet!' said I, `thing of evil! - prophet still, if bird or devil! -

Whether tempter sent, or whether tempest tossed thee here ashore,

Desolate yet all undaunted, on this desert land enchanted -

On this home by horror haunted - tell me truly, I implore -

Is there - is there balm in Gilead? - tell me - tell me, I implore!'

Quoth the raven, `Nevermore.'

<u>Stanza16</u>

`Prophet!' said I, `thing of evil! - prophet still, if bird or devil!

By that Heaven that bends above us - by that God we both adore -

Tell this soul with sorrow laden if, within the distant Aidenn,

It shall clasp a sainted maiden whom the angels named Lenore -

Clasp a rare and radiant maiden, whom the angels named Lenore?'

Quoth the raven, `Nevermore.'

Note:

1. A "tempest" is "a violent wind storm."

2. "Undaunted" means "courageous," or "not discouraged."

3. "Balm in Gilead" refers to "a soothing ointment made in Gilead," a mountainous region east of the Jordan river in the Middle East.

4. "Aidenn" is an Arabic word for "Eden," or "paradise" (heaven).

Part B - Poetry

Directions: Answer the questions below about the section of "The Raven" shown in Part A.

1. The first lines of both stanza 15 and 16 are the same. The narrator sees the raven as a sign of something. Whether the raven is a devil in the form of a bird, or just a bird, the narrator says the raven is what two things?

_____

2. What horror is haunting the home of the narrator?

_____

3. By this point, the narrator knows the raven will give the same answer, no matter what question the narrator asks. What question does the narrator ask in stanza 15?

_____

4. What might that question and answer mean, given especially that the narrator knew the raven's answer before he asked the question?

    a. The narrator didn't believe that the people of Gilead made a soothing ointment or balm.

    b. The narrator just wondered if the raven would keep giving the same answer.

    c. The narrator really was asking if there is anything that will soothe his pain from losing Lenore.

5. What is a short way of asking the question that the narrator asks in Stanza 16?

_____

6. The narrator is torturing himself with grief in the poem, and in stanzas 15 and 16 in particular. What evidence do the stanzas provide to support the idea of self-torture?

_____

_____

Part C- Summarize Passage

Directions: Read the passage and then follow the directions.

As you read in Lesson 38, rain can cause erosion of the soil. The *lack* of rain can also have the same effect.

A terrible drought took place in 1934 and 1935. During that time, severe wind erosion of the land took place on farms in Texas, Oklahoma, Kansas, Nebraska, Colorado, and the Dakotas. Many months passed without a drop of rain. The crops dried up and died in the fields. The soil got so dry that the wind blew it away. It was not uncommon to have clouds of dirt so gigantic that the sky would turn dark in the middle of the day. People wore handkerchiefs over their mouths to keep from choking on all the dirt in the air. Farm equipment, buildings, and even barbed-wire fences were buried under the dust. These dry and windy conditions went on for so long that the Great Plains area soon became known as the Dust Bowl.

Today, modern farming methods help to preserve the land in the Great Plains, and to conserve water. Although farmers need rain, they are able to withstand a drought like that of 1934-35 much better today than in the past.

Write a summary list for this passage.

Summary List:

_____

_____

_____

_____

Finally, use the list to help you write a short summary of the passage, in your own words. A summary should be two or three sentences long.

_____

_____

_____

_____

Part D - Main Idea

Directions: In the statements below, an *X* is placed next to three details from the passage in Part C. The letters *TG* are placed next to the choice that is too general to be a good title for the passage. Beside the letters *MI*, write a main idea statement for the passage.

X Clouds of dust were huge enough to block out the daylight.

X The drought of 1934-1935 was so severe, the area suffering from it became known as the Dust Bowl.

TG The Dirty Thirties

X Modern farming techniques have helped farmers withstand droughts like that of 1934-1935.

MI

_____

_____

Part E - Review

Directions: Using information from the flyer below, answer the questions.

Sixth Grade Spring Field Trip

Dear Families,

On Tuesday, May 26, our class will be taking a trip to the annual State Hands On Science Fair in Thomasville. We will be traveling by school bus and will be loaded and ready to leave the school at 8:00 a.m. SHARP! We plan to return to school by the end of the regularly scheduled day. Each student should bring a bagged lunch.

Please talk with your child and help them decide on TWO sessions they would like to attend. Enclose a check or cash to cover the cost of attending these sessions. The signed form and money should be returned to me no later than Friday, May 22nd. If you have any questions, please do not hesitate to call.

Thank you,
Mr. Johnson   555-1234

Sign-Up Form Title	Time	Cost
___ Underwater Submarine Ride	9:00 – 11:00	$4.00
___ Seashell Necklace	10:00-11:00	$2.00
___ Sailboat Building	9:00 – 11:00	$10.00
___ Pool Snorkeling	9:00 – 11:00	$10.00
___ Robot Pump	11:00 – 2:00	$15.00
___ Experiments You Won't Believe	1:00-2:00	$5.00
___ Your Body: A Virtual Tour	12:00 – 2:00	$5.00

Total: _____

_____
Name   Phone

Method of Payment
___ Cash
___ Check

_____
Parent or Guardian Signature   Date

1. Which of the following events is **not** held from 9:00-11:00?

   a. Underwater Submarine Ride

   b. Robot Romp

   c. Sailboat Building

   d. Pool Snorkeling

2. When is the last date the flyer can be returned to Mr. Johnson?

   a. Tuesday, May 26th

   b. the day of the field trip

   c. Monday, May 25th

   d. Friday, May 22nd

3. The flyer doesn't give you a reason, but why would it be important for a student and her parent or guardian to decide together which sessions to sign up for?

   _____

   _____

4. Which of the following did Mr. Johnson include in the flyer to let everyone know they should not be late on the day of the field trip?

   a. ...**no later**

   b. SHARP!

   c. ...will be loaded and ready to leave by 8:00

   d. If you have any questions...

5. There is enough information in this flyer to let you know that:

   a. You can collect real seashells to use in the "Seashell Necklace" session.

   b. "Experiments You Won't Believe!" is a new session this year.

   c. "Your Body: Virtual Tour" is the most popular session.

   d. You should eat your lunch before attending the "Robot Romp" session.

Part F - Bonus

Many times, poets use **partial rhymes**. Words that end with similar—but not exactly the same—sounds are **partial rhymes**.

Here are some examples of **partial rhymes**: rich and watch, bait and bit.

BONUS REVIEW

Here is a familiar verse:

> Hickory, dickory, dock,
>
> The mouse ran up the clock.
>
> The clock struck one,
>
> The mouse ran down!
>
> Hickory, dickory, dock.

The **rhyming pattern** of this nursery rhyme is: a a b c a.

Notice that the third and fourth lines end with **partial rhymes**: one and down.

Lesson 41

Part A - Poetry

By stanza 15 of "The Raven," the narrator is fairly certain that no matter what question he asks, the raven will give the same answer. He first asks if there is balm in Gilead, already knowing the answer. A balm, an ointment, soothes pain. The narrator thinks that nothing will soothe the pain he is feeling from the loss of Lenore. In stanza 16, the narrator asks if Lenore is in heaven, again knowing the answer the raven will give in advance. The narrator is being very negative, assuming the worst and then setting up the raven to make the worst seem true. In these stanzas, the narrator is not certain whether the raven is an evil prophet, maybe just a bird, or maybe a devil.

Below are the final two stanzas of "The Raven."

<u>Stanza 17</u>

'Be that word our sign of parting, bird or fiend!' I shrieked upstarting -

`Get thee back into the tempest and the Night's Plutonian shore!

Leave no black plume as a token of that lie thy soul hath spoken!

Leave my loneliness unbroken! - quit the bust above my door!

Take thy beak from out my heart, and take thy form from off my door!'

Quoth the raven, `Nevermore.'

<u>Stanza 18</u>

And the raven, never flitting, still is sitting, still is sitting

On the pallid bust of Pallas just above my chamber door;

And his eyes have all the seeming of a demon's that is dreaming,

And the lamp-light o'er him streaming throws his shadow on the floor;

And my soul from out that shadow that lies floating on the floor

Shall be lifted - nevermore!

Part B- Poetry

Directions: Answer the questions about the section of "The Raven" shown in Part A.

1. At the beginning of stanza 17, when the narrator says, "Be that word our sign of parting," what word is he referring to?

    _____

2. The narrator is suddenly very angry at the raven because:

    a.   The raven said in Stanza 16 that Lenore isn't in heaven.

    b.   The narrator is tired of having a bird in his bedroom.

    c.   The raven has gotten his beak stuck in the narrator's heart.

3. What line in Stanza 17 tells us that the narrator doesn't believe what the raven has said about Lenore not being in heaven?

    _____

    _____

4. Tell briefly what stanza 17 is about.

    _____

    _____

5. Tell briefly what stanza 18 is about.

    _____

    _____

Part C- Summarize Passage

Directions: Read the passage and then follow the directions.

In Punxsutawney, Pennsylvania, the town's official mascot plays an important part in one of the town's most famous traditions. Every year, Punxsutawney Phil emerges from his hole on February 2nd. If he sees his shadow, everyone can expect six more weeks of winter. If he doesn't see his shadow, spring must be close behind. It is weather lore with deep roots. Believe it or not, it may even be based on science.

Centuries ago in Europe, February 2nd, also known as Candlemas Day, was a meaningful day. People lit candles to drive away evil spirits. They also watched the behavior of bears and other mammals that usually hibernated during the winter. On a clear day, animals emerged from their dens and saw their shadow. They would become frightened and quickly return to the safety of their dens. A cloudy day was seen as a sign that spring was near because there were no shadows and the animals would not go back to their dens. February 2nd was also a handy date for farmers hoping to estimate how many weeks of winter remained.

Can this rodent's shadow, or lack of a shadow, actually involve science? Possibly. After living underground for months, a groundhog's eyes are probably sensitive to bright light, so sunlight will likely send it right back into its burrow. On a dark overcast day, it might be a good time for the groundhog to stretch its muscles and check out what's going on in the outside world.

Regarding the weather, there may be some truth in the groundhog tradition. Clear skies and sunshine probably mean a dry and stable pattern. This happens when a cold Arctic air mass is stalled in the atmosphere. Long periods of cold weather usually follow. Overcast skies could mean that warm, moist air is approaching, and spring may not be too far behind.

Write a summary list for this passage.

Summary List:

_____

_____

_____

_____

Finally, use the list to help you write a short summary of the passage, in your own words.
A summary should be two or three sentences long.

_____

_____

_____

_____

Part D - Main Idea

Directions: In the statements below, an _X_ is placed next to three details from the passage in Part C. The letters _TG_ are placed next to the statement that would be too general to be a main idea statement. Beside the letters _MI,_ write a main idea statement for the passage.

_TG_ February 2nd is a day traditionally used to predict the remaining weeks of winter weather.

_X_ In Europe, candles were lit to drive away evil spirits on Candlemas Day.

_X_ On a cloudy day, animals may stay out of their dens longer because their eyes are sensitive to light.

_X_ A stalled cold mass will usually signal that long periods of cold weather will follow.

_MI_

_____

_____

Part E - Review

Directions: Re-read the passage in Part C, and then answer the questions.

1. Which of the following is the best possible meaning for the underlined word in the model sentence?

    Model: It is weather <u>lore</u> with deep roots.

    a. conditions

    b. science

    c. tradition

    d. evidence

2. When our eyes become sensitive to light we usually respond by doing what?

    a. putting on sunglasses

    b. shading our eyes by wearing a hat

    c. squinting

    d. all of the above

3. Look at the underlined word in the model sentence. Choose the sentence that uses the underlined word in the same way as the model sentence.

    Model: If he doesn't see his shadow, <u>spring</u> must be close behind.

    a. An underground <u>spring</u> has supplied our well with cool, clear water for years.

    b. Last night a <u>spring</u> on my bed broke and popped right up through the mattress!

    c. I know everyone enjoys <u>spring</u>, but for me it means watery eyes and a runny nose from all the pollen in the air.

    d. You must be feeling better today because I notice a <u>spring</u> in your step.

4. The passage doesn't tell you the answer, but which of the following statements about February 2nd is a fact?

    a. February 2nd will fall on a different day of the week depending on the year.

    b. A groundhog is the only animal that can be used for this unscientific experiment.

    c. Groundhog Day is the most important tradition in Pennsylvania.

    d. If a groundhog sees its shadow, there will be at least six more weeks of cold winter weather.

5. Using information from the passage, which of the following would best fit in the empty box of the chart below?

    a. The groundhog is frightened by its shadow.

    b. The groundhog stays outside, signaling spring is soon to follow.

    c. Farmers will need to wait a while longer to plant their crops.

    d. An arctic air mass will bring more cold weather.

6. Circle the box that gives the scientific explanation for the coming of spring.

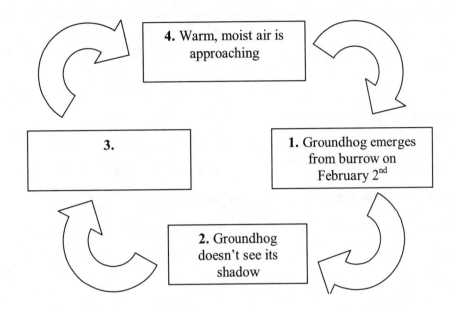

Part F - Bonus

Look at the words in **BOLD** from three lines of "The Raven."

> Once upon a midnight **dreary**, while I pondered weak and **weary**,
>
> Over many a quaint and curious volume of forgotten lore,
>
> While I nodded, nearly **napping**, suddenly there came a **tapping**,

You know that in many poems, words at the ends of the lines in stanzas often rhyme. The bold words in the example show **internal rhymes**. An **internal rhyme** is a word within a line that rhymes with another word at the end of the line.

Part G– Bonus

Here are words that tell how many **metrical feet** are in a line of poetry:

quatrameter: four metrical feet

pentameter: five metrical feet

octameter: eight metrical feet

These words might seem to be difficult, but they aren't. "Quatra" is related to the word quarter and means four. "Penta" means five, as in a pentagon. "Octa" means eight and is related closely to the word octopus.

Lesson 42

Part A- Poetry

Directions: Follow your teacher's instructions.

<u>Stanza 1</u>

Once upon a midnight dreary, while I pondered weak and weary,

Over many a quaint and curious volume of forgotten lore,

While I nodded, nearly napping, suddenly there came a tapping,

As of some one gently rapping, rapping at my chamber door.

`'Tis some visitor,' I muttered, `tapping at my chamber door -

Only this, and nothing more.'

<u>Stanza 2</u>

Ah, distinctly I remember it was in the bleak December,

And each separate dying ember wrought its ghost upon the floor.

Eagerly I wished the morrow; - vainly I had sought to borrow

From my books surcease of sorrow - sorrow for the lost Lenore -

For the rare and radiant maiden whom the angels named Lenore-

Nameless here for evermore.

<u>Stanza 3</u>

And the silken sad uncertain rustling of each purple curtain

Thrilled me - filled me with fantastic terrors never felt before;

So that now, to still the beating of my heart, I stood repeating

`'Tis some visitor entreating entrance at my chamber door -

Some late visitor entreating entrance at my chamber door; -

This it is, and nothing more,'

Stanza 4

Presently my heart grew stronger; hesitating then no longer,

`Sir,' said I, `or Madam, truly your forgiveness I implore;

But the fact is I was napping, and so gently you came rapping,

And so faintly you came tapping, tapping at my chamber door,

That I scarce was sure I heard you' - here I opened wide the door; -

Darkness there, and nothing more.

Stanza 5

Deep into that darkness peering, long I stood there wondering, fearing,

Doubting, dreaming dreams no mortal ever dared to dream to dream before

But the silence was unbroken, and the darkness gave no token,

And the only word there spoken was the whispered word, `Lenore!'

This I whispered, and an echo murmured back the word, `Lenore!'

Merely this and nothing more.

Stanza 6

Back into the chamber turning, all my soul within me burning,

Soon again I heard a tapping somewhat louder than before.

`Surely,' said I, `surely that is something at my window lattice;

Let me see then, what the threat is, and this mystery explore -

Let my heart be still a moment and this mystery explore; -

'Tis the wind and nothing more!'

Stanza 7

Open here I flung the shutter, when, with many a flirt and flutter,

In there stepped a stately raven of the saintly days of yore.

Not the least obeisance made he; not an instant stopped or stayed he;

But, with mien of lord or lady, perched above my chamber door -

Perched upon a bust of Pallas just above my chamber door -

Perched, and sat, and nothing more.

Stanza 8

Then this ebony bird beguiling my sad fancy into smiling,

By the grave and stern decorum of the countenance it wore,

`Though thy crest be shorn and shaven, thou,' I said, `art sure no craven.

Ghastly grim and ancient raven wandering from the nightly shore -

Tell me what thy lordly name is on the Night's Plutonian shore!'

Quoth the raven, `Nevermore.'

Stanza 9

Much I marveled this ungainly fowl to hear discourse so plainly,

Though its answer little meaning - little relevancy bore;

For we cannot help agreeing that no living human being

Ever yet was blessed with seeing bird above his chamber door -

Bird or beast above the sculptured bust above his chamber door,

With such name as `Nevermore.'

Stanza 10

But the raven, sitting lonely on the placid bust, spoke only,

That one word, as if his soul in that one word he did outpour.

Nothing further then he uttered - not a feather then he fluttered -

Till I scarcely more than muttered `Other friends have flown before -

On the morrow will he leave me, as my hopes have flown before.'

Then the bird said, `Nevermore.'

Part B - Summarize Passage

Directions: Read the passage and then follow the directions.

Whether it be reciting the popular nursery rhyme "Twinkle, Twinkle Little Star," or gazing up at the sky on a cloudless night, the twinkling quality of the stars will always delight us. Exactly why do these tiny dots appear to sparkle like diamonds?

Starlight must pass through the Earth's atmosphere before it reaches your eyes. As it does, it comes into contact with some places where the air is warm, and other places where the air is cold. This causes the star's light to be bent. Depending on how the light is bent, sometimes only a little starlight reaches your eye, and the star looks dim. Other times, more starlight reaches your eye, and the star looks brighter. Because the amount of light changes quickly, the star appears to twinkle.

In contrast to stars, the planets usually do not twinkle. The planets are too close to the Earth to show up as only points of light. Because they are so close, light from different parts of the planet continuously reaches your eye. This makes the planets seem to shine with a steady light.

Write a summary list for this passage.

Summary List:

_____

_____

_____

_____

Finally, use the list to help you write a short summary of the passage, in your own words.
A summary should be two or three sentences long.

_____

_____

_____

_____

Part C - Main Idea

Directions: In the statements below, an *X* is placed next to three details from the passage in Part B. The letters *TG* are placed next to the statement that would be too general to be a main idea statement. Beside the letters *MI*, write a main idea statement for the passage.

TG Stars twinkle and planets shine based on how far away from the earth they are.

X Different places in the atmosphere vary in temperature.

X Planets are closer to the earth than stars.

X The amount of starlight we see depends on the temperature of the atmosphere it passes through.

MI

_____

_____

Part D - Review

Directions: Refer to the poem "The Raven" to answer the following question.

1.   What is the name of the woman who is mourned by the narrator?

_____

Directions: Use the chart below to answer the questions.

March MENU

APPETIZERS
Fried Cheese Sticks: $1.00

Zesty Chicken Wings (10): $1.50

Stringy Cheese Bread: $1.00

Jumbo Fried Onion Rings: $1.75

Assorted Vegetables and Dip: $1.00

SALADS
One Time Visit Salad Bar: $1.50

Crunchy Apple Waldorf Salad: $.75

ENTREES: $2.00
Cheesy Macaroni and Cheese w/ Small Salad

Hamburger with Fries

Peanut Butter & Jelly Sandwich w/Baked Chips

Taco Bar / Cheese or Pepperoni Pizza Slices (2)

DESSERTS

Assorted Fresh Fruit: $.50

BEVERAGES: $.50

Milk- White or Chocolate

Assorted Fruit Juices

Bottled Water

2. The setting for this menu is probably a:

    a. fast food drive-through

    b. school cafeteria

    c. amusement park snack bar

    d. family home

3. Which of the following words in the menu tell you that there is a variety to choose from?

    a. one time

    b. with

    c. and

    d. assorted

4. Which of the following is the best definition for the underlined word in the model phrase from the menu?
Model: One Time Visit Salad <u>Bar</u>

    a. the legal profession

    b. a counter where a variety of things are served

    c. an oblong piece or block of something

    d. a vertical line across a musical staff marking equal measures of time

5. You can buy all of the following beverages **except**:

    a. bottled water

    b. fruit juice

    c. lemonade

    d. white or chocolate milk

6. List at least *three* words from the menu that describe some type of food.

_____

7. What are the two items that have something else included with them? (Note: There are **TWO** correct answers.)

    a. Cheesy Macaroni and Cheese

    b. Taco Bar

    c. Peanut Butter & Jelly Sandwich

    d. Stringy Cheese Bread

8. How many items can you purchase for $1.00 or less?

    a. 8

    b. 3

    c. 5

    d. 10

Part E- Bonus Review

These words tell how many **metrical feet** are in a line of poetry:

quatrameter: four metrical feet

pentameter: five metrical feet

octameter: eight metrical feet

An **internal rhyme** is a word within a line that rhymes with another word at the end of the line.

Example: Much I marveled this **ungainly** fowl to hear discourse so **plainly**

Lesson 43

Part A - Poetry

Directions: Follow your teacher's instructions.

Stanza 11

Startled at the stillness broken by reply so aptly spoken,

`Doubtless,' said I, `what it utters is its only stock and store,

Caught from some unhappy master whom unmerciful disaster

Followed fast and followed faster till his songs one burden bore -

Till the dirges of his hope that melancholy burden bore

Of "Never-nevermore."

Stanza 12

But the raven still beguiling all my sad soul into smiling,

Straight I wheeled a cushioned seat in front of bird and bust and door;

Then, upon the velvet sinking, I betook myself to linking

Fancy unto fancy, thinking what this ominous bird of yore -

What this grim, ungainly, gaunt, and ominous bird of yore

Meant in croaking `Nevermore.'

Stanza 13

This I sat engaged in guessing, but no syllable expressing

To the fowl whose fiery eyes now burned into my bosom's core;

This and more I sat divining, with my head at ease reclining

On the cushion's velvet violet lining that the lamp-light gloated o'er,

But whose velvet violet lining with the lamp-light gloating o'er,

She shall press, ah, nevermore!

Stanza 14

Then, methought, the air grew denser, perfumed from an unseen censer

Swung by angels whose faint foot-falls tinkled on the tufted floor.

`Wretch,' I cried, `thy God hath lent thee - by these angels he has sent thee

Respite - respite and nepenthe from the memories of Lenore!

Quaff, oh quaff this kind nepenthe, and forget this lost Lenore!'

Quoth the raven, `Nevermore.'

Stanza 15

`Prophet!' said I, `thing of evil! - prophet still, if bird or devil! -

Whether tempter sent, or whether tempest tossed thee here ashore,

Desolate yet all undaunted, on this desert land enchanted -

On this home by horror haunted - tell me truly, I implore -

Is there - is there balm in Gilead? - tell me - tell me, I implore!'

Quoth the raven, `Nevermore.'

Stanza 16

`Prophet!' said I, `thing of evil! - prophet still, if bird or devil!

By that Heaven that bends above us-by that God we both adore-

Tell this soul with sorrow laden if, within the distant Aidenn,

It shall clasp a sainted maiden whom the angels named Lenore -

Clasp a rare and radiant maiden, whom the angels named Lenore?'

Quoth the raven, `Nevermore.'

Stanza 17

`Be that word our sign of parting, bird or fiend!' I shrieked upstarting -

`Get thee back into the tempest and the Night's Plutonian shore!

Leave no black plume as a token of that lie thy soul hath spoken!

Leave my loneliness unbroken! - quit the bust above my door!

Take thy beak from out my heart, and take thy form from off my door!'

Quoth the raven, `Nevermore.'

Stanza 18

And the raven, never flitting, still is sitting, still is sitting

On the pallid bust of Pallas just above my chamber door;

And his eyes have all the seeming of a demon's that is dreaming,

And the lamp-light o'er him streaming throws his shadow on the floor;

And my soul from out that shadow that lies floating on the floor

Shall be lifted - nevermore!

Part B - Summarize Passage

Directions: Read the passage and then follow the directions.

A symbol that stands for a number is called a *numeral*. The number symbols used centuries ago by the Romans are called **Roman numerals**.

There are seven basic Roman numerals. The seven basic numerals are: I, V, X, L, C, D, and M. I stands for 1, V stands for 5, X stands for 10, L stands for 50, C stands for 100, D stands for 500, and M stands for 1000. All other numbers are shown by combinations of these numerals. The numbers are written from left to right and are usually formed by adding numerals together. Sixteen, for example, is

X + V + I = XVI

10 + 5 + 1 = 16

Some Roman numerals are formed by using subtraction. For example, instead of adding four ones to make four (IIII) the Romans usually subtracted 1 from 5, writing IV. Using this general rule, the Romans were able to simplify many numbers. Examples are: writing IX instead of VIIII for 9, and CD instead of CCCC for 400.

No one has been able to find the original source of the Roman numerals. There are two main thoughts about how V came to stand for 5. Some scholars say that five was first shown by holding up one hand with the thumb held apart from the fingers. The hand was imitated in drawings, and was later simplified to V. Five could also be represented by half the X (10), or V.

Roman numerals are easy to use when you want to add or subtract numbers, but multiplication and division are much harder. Today, the Roman system is used to number the faces of clocks, to list topics in outlines, to record dates on monuments and public buildings, and in other limited circumstances.

Write a summary list for this passage.

Summary List:

_____

_____

_____

_____

Finally, use the list to help you write a short summary of the passage, in your own words.

A summary should be two or three sentences long.

_____

_____

_____

_____

Part C- Main Idea

Directions: In the statements below, an *X* is placed next to three details from the passage in Part B. The letters *TG* are placed next to the statement that would be too general to be a main idea statement. Beside the letters *MI* write a main idea statement for the passage.

TG The uses of Roman numerals are limited.

X There are seven basic Roman numerals.

X Addition and subtraction are easier than multiplication and division with Roman numerals.

X Clocks, dates on buildings, and parts of a written outline are common uses of Roman numerals today.

MI _____

_____

Part D- Review

Directions: Refer to the poem "The Raven" to answer the following question.

1. The word "nevermore" is rarely used any more. What does it mean?

_____

Directions: Read the passage below and answer the questions.

If you look down at our planet from outer space, most of what you see is water; 71% of the

planet's surface, or about 140 million square miles, is covered by ocean and it is because of this that the Earth is sometimes called *"the water planet."* Only about three-tenths of our globe is covered with land. The oceans contain roughly 97% of the Earth's water supply.

The oceans of Earth are <u>unique</u> in our Solar System. No other planet in our Solar System has liquid water (although recent finds on Mars indicate that Mars may have had some liquid water in the recent past).

The oceans of Earth serve many functions, especially affecting the weather and temperature. They moderate the Earth's temperature by absorbing incoming solar radiation (stored as heat energy). The always-moving ocean currents distribute this heat energy around the globe. This heats the land and air during winter and cools it during summer.

Until the year 2000, there were four recognized oceans: the Pacific, Atlantic, Indian, and Arctic. In the Spring of 2000, the International Hydrographic Organization delimited a new ocean, the Southern Ocean, it surrounds Antarctica. These oceans, although distinct in some ways, are all interconnected; the same water is circulated throughout them all.

There are also many seas (smaller branches of an ocean); seas are often partly enclosed by land. The largest seas are the South China Sea, the Caribbean Sea, and the Mediterranean Sea.

2. Which of the following sentences expresses the author's specific purpose?

    a. The author's purpose is to persuade the reader that Mars used to have liquid water.

    b. The author's purpose is to inform the reader about the world's oceans.

    c. The author's purpose is to entertain the reader with a story about the International Hydrographic Organization.

    d. The author's purpose is to inform the reader about our Solar System.

3. Distinct means:

    a. the same as one another

    b. interconnected

    c. different from one another

    d. enclosed

4. A good title for this passage would be:

    a. Water, Water Everywhere!

    b. The New Ocean

    c. Water on Mars?

    d. The History of the International Hydrographic Organization

5. There is enough information in this story to show:

    a. The Earth is called "the water planet" for a good reason.

    b. The Pacific Ocean is the largest ocean.

    c. The Atlantic Ocean borders the US to the east.

    d. It took years to delimit the new Southern Ocean.

6. What do you call a smaller branch of an ocean?

    a. unique

    b. a current

    c. a sea

    d. a moderator

7. Which of the following is the best possible meaning for the underlined word in the model sentence?

    Model: The oceans of Earth are <u>unique</u> in our Solar System.

    a. one of a kind

    b. common

    c. beautiful

    d. large

Part E- Bonus Review

A **cognitive map** is a representation of someone's thinking

Each of the following words could be a **trochaic foot** in a poem:
    fa´ther la´yer wi´nter no´tebook fru´strate

A **pentameter** line of poetry has five **metrical feet**.

Lesson 44

Part A - Poetry

Directions: Follow your teacher's instructions.

"The Raven" is a good example of why people write poetry. It is clear in the poem that the narrator is mourning the loss of Lenore--perhaps the narrator's wife or fiancée.

Different types of artists have dealt with the theme of the loss of a loved one. Many popular and country songs over the years have been about couples breaking up, for example.

Think about this discussion question: Why did Edgar Allen Poe write a poem about this topic? Why didn't he write an essay about losing someone, instead? Why didn't he write just one sentence, such as, "I lost the love of my life and now I'm very depressed and upset?" What has Poe accomplished in "The Raven" that would be difficult to accomplish in any other way?

Part B - Summarize Passage

Directions: Read the passage and then follow the directions.

The first radios were used by ships to communicate with other ships, or with people on the shore. The first radios were called "wireless." The Metropolitan Opera House in New York City created an experimental broadcasting program in 1910, and the University of Wisconsin began operating an experimental radio station in 1915.

Beginning in 1925, and for the next 25 years, radio became the primary source of entertainment for families. Radios, like televisions today, were affordable and almost everyone had one. Families would gather around the radio every night and listen to their favorite programs. There were a variety of shows to listen to, such as comedy, daily soap operas, dramas, action/adventure shows, and of course music. Because of radio, almost everyone was able to listen to the music of great band leaders popular during that time.

President Franklin D. Roosevelt used radio broadcasts to speak to the people of the United States about government policy. These popular radio addresses were known as "fireside chats." During World War II, radio newscasts made it possible to keep Americans informed about the progress of the war.

Write a summary list for this passage.

Summary List:

_____

_____

_____

_____

Finally, use the list to help you write a short summary of the passage, in your own words.
A summary should be two or three sentences long.

_____

_____

_____

_____

Part C - Main Idea

Directions: In the statements below, an *X* is placed next to three details from the passage in Part B. The letters *TG* are placed next to the statement that would be too general to be a main idea statement. Beside the letters *MI*, write a main idea statement for the passage.

TG Radios are used in a variety of ways.

X Families listened to a variety of programs and music for entertainment.

X The first radios were used aboard ships.

X The Metropolitan Opera House in New York City created an experimental broadcasting program in 1910.

MI

_____

_____

Part D - Review

Directions: Read the passage below and then answer the questions.

An isthmus is a narrow strip of land that connects larger bodies of land. Some isthmuses connect two continents. The Isthmus of Panama links North America and South America. Others join a continent to a peninsula.

Panama is an S-shaped country in Central America that lies between Costa Rica and Colombia. The Isthmus of Panama is a narrow neck of land that separates the Atlantic and Pacific oceans. That small piece of land has long been used as a bridge between South America and North America. For centuries, it frustrated explorers as an annoying, narrow barrier between the Atlantic and Pacific oceans.

Because an isthmus is narrow, it is a logical place to dig a canal between the two bodies of water it separates. The United States built the Panama Canal in 1914. Thousands of laborers worked on the canal for about 10 years. Steam shovels and other types of machinery were used to cut through jungles, hills, and swamps. The work was difficult, and the workers had to overcome tropical diseases such as malaria and yellow fever.

People sailing from New York City to San Francisco enjoyed a much shorter trip by being able to cut across the Isthmus of Panama to get from the Atlantic Ocean to the Pacific Ocean. Previously, ships making this trip had to travel around South America, which more than doubled the distance. As an another example, the Suez Canal, through the isthmus between Africa and Asia, cut the distance between England and India by about 5,000 miles.

1. In the first paragraph the word "others" refers to:

    a. continents

    b. countries

    c. isthmuses

    d. bodies of water

2. Which of the following sentences expresses the author's specific purpose?

    a. The author's purpose is to persuade the reader that the existence of an isthmus made traveling and exploring a frustrating experience.

    b. The author's purpose is to explain to the reader how the Panama Canal was built.

    c. The author's purpose is to entertain the reader with a story about traveling from New York to San Francisco.

    d. The author's purpose is to define an isthmus and to explain the benefits of digging a canal through one, using the Panama Canal as an example.

3. All of the following would be an example of a <u>barrier</u> **except**:

    a. fence

    b. a roadblock

    c. an open door

    d. a barricade

4. Which situation would best compare to the effect an isthmus has on travel?

    a. walking up or down the stairs instead of the riding the elevator

    b. waiting in a long, slow moving line to buy movie tickets

    c. driving extra miles following a detour route because of road construction

    d. running instead of walking somewhere

5. Briefly describe the conditions the laborers faced while building the Panama canal.

_____

_____

_____

6. Which of the following titles BEST tells what this passage is about?

    a. Natural Bridges

    b. Breaking the Barrier

    c. The Quickest Way to Travel

    d. Panama Changes Forever

Part E - Bonus Review

A **cognitive map** is a representation of someone's thinking. Here is a simple **cognitive map**:

An **octameter** line of poetry has eight **metrical feet**.

Here are some examples of **partial rhymes**: late and flat; wish and wash, wish and which.

Lesson 45 Homework

Directions: Follow your teacher's instructions.

The Chimney Sweeper.

When my mother died I was very young,
And my father sold me while yet my tongue,
Could scarcely cry weep weep weep weep.
So your chimneys I sweep & in soot I sleep.

There's little Tom Dacre, who cried when his head
That curl'd like a lambs back, was shav'd, so I said
'Hush Tom never mind it, for when your head's bare,

You know that the soot cannot spoil your white hair.'

And so he was quiet, & that very night,
As Tom was a sleeping he had such a sight!-
That thousands of sweepers Dick, Joe, Ned & Jack
Were all of them lock'd up in coffins of black.

And by came an Angel who had a bright key,
And he open'd the coffins & set them all free;
Then down a green plain leaping laughing they run
And wash in a river and shine in the Sun.

Then naked & white, all their bags left behind,
They rise upon clouds, and sport in the wind;
And the Angel told Tom if he'd be a good boy,
He'd have God for his father & never want joy.

And so Tom awoke and we rose in the dark,
And got with our bags & our brushes to work.
Tho' the morning was cold, Tom was happy & warm;
So if all do their duty, they need not fear harm.

Lesson 46

Part A - Poetry

First, look at the first stanza below from "The Raven."

Stanza 1

Once upon a midnight dreary, while I pondered weak and weary,

Over many a quaint and curious volume of forgotten lore,

> While I nodded, nearly napping, suddenly there came a tapping,
>
> As of some one gently rapping, rapping at my chamber door.
>
> `'Tis some visitor,' I muttered, `tapping at my chamber door -
>
> Only this, and nothing more.'

The first line has an **internal rhyme**. That is, the word **dreary** in the middle of the line rhymes with the word **weary** at the end of the line.

The third line, like the first, has an **internal rhyme**. The word **napping** in the middle of the line rhymes with the word **tapping** at the end of the line.

None of the other lines has an **internal rhyme**.

Note that there are six lines in the first stanza. The first five of those lines have eight **trochaic feet**. Lines with **eight metrical feet** are called **octameter lines**. The sixth line has only **four trochaic feet**. Lines with **four metrical feet** are called **quatrameter lines**.

Part B - Poetry

Directions: After you read the second stanza of "The Raven," answer the questions. You may look at Part A to help you answer the questions.

<u>Stanza 2</u>

> Ah, distinctly I remember it was in the bleak December,
>
> And each separate dying ember wrought its ghost upon the floor.
>
> Eagerly I wished the morrow; - vainly I had sought to borrow
>
> From my books surcease of sorrow - sorrow for the lost Lenore -
>
> For the rare and radiant maiden whom the angels named Lenore-
>
> Nameless here for evermore.

1. The first and third lines of this stanza have **internal rhymes**. Which words rhyme in those lines?

first line: _____

third line: _____

2. Are there any internal rhymes in lines 2, 4, 5, or 6?

_____

3. Which line is a quatrameter line?

_____

4. What type of lines are lines 1-5, which each have eight **trochaic feet**?

_____

5. Which word below is a **trochaic metrical foot** by itself? Remember, a trochaic metrical foot has one stressed syllable, followed by one unstressed syllable.

    a. believe

    b. remember

    c. dying

Part C - Paraphrase Paragraph

When you **paraphrase** a sentence, you rewrite the sentence in your own words. When you **paraphrase** a paragraph, you rewrite the whole paragraph in your own words.

Read the paragraph below:

> A terrible drought took place in 1934 and 1935. Many months passed without a drop of rain. The soil got so dry that the wind blew it away. During that time, severe wind erosion of the land took place on the farms in Texas, Oklahoma, Kansas, Nebraska, Colorado and the Dakotas. It was not uncommon to have clouds of dirt so gigantic that the sky would turn dark in the middle of the day. The crops dried up and died in the fields. These dry and windy conditions went on for so long that the Great Plains area soon became known as the Dust Bowl.

Although it is not especially easy to **paraphrase** an entire paragraph, you can make it easier if you first outline the structure of the paragraph. Here is one way to outline the structure of the paragraph above:

A. About: drought of 1934 and 1935

1. Detail: didn't rain
2. Detail: dry soil blew away
3. Detail: severe wind erosion
4. Detail: huge clouds of dust
5. Detail: crops died

B. Summary: Great Plains area was called Dust Bowl

The best way to paraphrase a paragraph is to base your paraphrase on the paragraph structure. You should write about the ideas in the structure, using your own words.

Part D - Paraphrase Passage

Directions: Paraphrase the paragraph in Part C. Write about the parts of the paragraph structure, using your own words.

_____

_____

_____

_____

_____

Part E - Review

Directions: Read the passage and then follow the directions.

A dam is a barrier placed across a river to stop the flow of water. Dams can be made from earth or rocks and they can be quite small. They can also be made of concrete and rise as high as a skyscraper. People have always had to gather water during wet seasons to have enough for themselves, their animals, and their crops during dry spells.

Dams create lakes (called **reservoirs**) for storing water and providing it when it is needed. Dams also help prevent floods by storing floodwaters. The stored water can later be used to irrigate fields or to increase the flow of a stream for fish and wildlife during the dry season. Dams also store drinking water for people, and water for use by industries and cities. The lakes created by dams are used for recreation, and they provide a sanctuary for water birds.

Throughout history, when people decided where to settle, they looked for water. An important first concern was to locate a water supply large enough to fill their needs. In many areas, streams can be full of water during certain seasons of the year, but they may become dry when water is needed the most. At first, people built small dams of brush, earth, and rock that would store enough water for immediate needs. But floods frequently washed these small dams away. As the demand for more water became greater, people learned to construct larger dams that could be counted on to provide the water they needed. These dams could store enough water to meet people's needs during the dry seasons of the year. They could also supply the water needed during periods of drought that lasted for several years. Later, people learned how to use the energy of falling water to produce electric power for homes and industries.

1. This story mainly shows:

 a. Dams provide a way to store water necessary to meet the needs of all life on earth.

 b. Water is important for recreation.

 c. Stored water is necessary to meet the electrical needs of homes and industries.

 d. Birds could not survive without lakes that are provided by dams.

2. Which of the following statements is an *opinion*?

 a. Electricity produced by water power is cheaper than electricity produced by wind power.

 b. Many birds return to the same body of water each year.

 c. Most people are wasteful in their use of water.

 d. Crops in the field need to be irrigated when there isn't enough rainfall.

3. According to the passage, what factor was most important in deciding where people were going to settle?

 a. closeness to neighbors

 b. adequate water supply

 c. enough trees to build shelter

 d. nearby forms of transportation

4. All of the following are important uses of stored water stated in the passage *except*:

 a. increase the flow of water in streams for fish and wildlife

 b. recreation

 c. supply water to other countries

 d. provide water for dry seasons or in years of drought

5. The passage doesn't actually tell you the answer, but what would probably be the main reason for an increase in the demand for water?

 a. a decrease in the amount of yearly rainfall

 b. more people are taking up boating or other forms of water recreation

 c. an increase in the number of birds that need shelter

 d. the growing number of communities, their population, and their needs

6.   Water used as the power to produce electricity may come from a:

    a.   tidal wave

    b.   faucet

    c.   large amount of flowing water released by a dam

    d.   large amount of runoff

Part F - Bonus

A **stanza** of a poem with four lines is called a **quatrain**.

A **stanza** of a poem with six lines is called a **sestet**.

All the **stanzas** in "The Raven" have six lines. Those **stanzas** are all **sestets**.

Quatrain and **quatrameter** can be confusing. Remember that meter means "to measure." A **quatrameter** is a measure of the number of **metrical feet** (such as **trochees**) in a line. A **quatrain** tells the number of lines in a **stanza**.

Lesson 47

Part A - Poetry

First, look at the third stanza of "The Raven" below.

    <u>Stanza 3</u>

    And the silken sad uncertain rustling of each purple curtain

    Thrilled me - filled me with fantastic terrors never felt before;

    So that now, to still the beating of my heart, I stood repeating

    `'Tis some visitor entreating entrance at my chamber door -

    Some late visitor entreating entrance at my chamber door; -

    This it is, and nothing more,'

There are **six lines** in this stanza. A stanza that has six lines is called a **sestet**.

Remember:

    a.   When one word within a line of poetry rhymes with another word in that line, the rhyming words are called an **internal rhyme**.

    b.   A **trochaic metrical foot** has one stressed syllable followed by one unstressed syllable.

    c.   Lines with **eight metrical feet** are called **octameter lines**.

d.   Lines with **four metrical feet** are called **quatrameter lines**.

Part B - Poetry

Directions: After you read the fourth stanza of "The Raven," answer the questions. You may look at Part A to help you answer the questions.

Stanza 4

Presently my heart grew stronger; hesitating then no longer,

`Sir,' said I, `or Madam, truly your forgiveness I implore;

But the fact is I was napping, and so gently you came rapping,

And so faintly you came tapping, tapping at my chamber door,

That I scarce was sure I heard you' - here I opened wide the door; -

Darkness there, and nothing more.

1.   The first and third lines of this stanza have **internal rhymes**. Which words rhyme in those lines?

first line: _____

third line: _____

2.   Are there any internal rhymes in line 5?

_____

3.   Which line is a quatrameter line?

_____

4.   Lines 1-5 are octameter lines, meaning they each have eight metrical feet. What kind of metrical feet do they have?

_____

5. Which word below is a **trochaic metrical foot** by itself? Remember, a trochaic metrical foot has one stressed syllable, followed by one unstressed syllable.

    a. forgiveness

    b. faintly

    c. scarce

6. This stanza is a sestet. That means it has what?

Part C - Paraphrase Paragraph

Directions: Paraphrase the paragraph below. The paragraph structure is provided for you in the chart below the paragraph. Write about the parts of the paragraph structure, using your own words.

A simple word like *for* has many different meanings. You can be *for* something, rather than against it. *For* can mean "in spite of," as in "He is a nice guy, *for* all the problems he has had." If a piece of equipment is *for* the Army, that means it is intended to be used by them. If you trade one type of card *for* another, then the word means to exchange. You can use *for* to express a wish, as in, "What I'd give *for* some chocolate ice cream about now." Actually, most words have more than one meaning, including simple words like *for*.

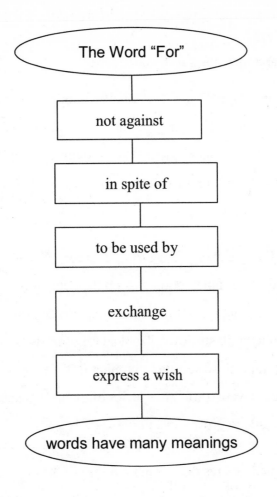

The Word "For"

not against

in spite of

to be used by

exchange

express a wish

words have many meanings

_____

_____

_____

_____

_____

Part D - Review

Directions: Read the passage and then answer the questions.

When most of us hear the word "desert" we usually think of hot dry places. But there are actually places called "cold deserts." Scientists define deserts as areas of land where less than ten inches of rain falls per year and few plants grow. These conditions apply to the arctic and Antarctic regions. The little amount of moisture that does fall is always frozen in the form of ice or snow, so plants can't use it to grow.

Most deserts are a result of weather patterns. For example, The Gobi Desert in Asia is cold for most of the year. In another example, mountains on the edge of deserts prevent rain from entering. The rain stays on the other side of the mountain, creating rain forests next to many deserts. These deserts are called rain shadows. Tropical rain forests have the greatest variety of plants and animals. Deserts run a close second in number of different species of plants and animals. While deserts have a several different species of plants, because of the harsh conditions, very few of those plants are able to grow and survive.

Deserts can also be created as a result of man's overuse of the land. Two thousand years ago a desert was created by people where there had been a forest before. During the time of the Roman Empire, the northern Sahara was ideal for farming. Forests were cut for firewood and to make fields. The land was plowed (turned over) so much of the soil was continuously exposed. The soil was blown away by the wind or washed away by the rain. Animals overgrazed the supply of grass which also exposed the soil. The loss of topsoil resulted in a <u>reduction</u> of plants that could grow. Because there were fewer plants to hold moisture, water evaporated quickly.

It's hard to imagine, but two thousand years is a relatively short time in the history of the earth. During that short time, the climate in the area changed from moist to dry. In this case, the desert was actually damaged land. But the activities that occurred during the Roman Empire are still going on in some places on the Earth.

1. This passage is mostly about:

    a.   the variety of plants and animals that live in the desert

    b.   the creation of natural deserts, and the continuing activities of man that can create "damaged land" deserts

    c.   tropical rain forests and deserts living side by side separated only by mountains

    d.   the deserts of the Arctic and Antarctic regions

2. Deserts are the result of which of the following? (Note: There are **TWO** correct answers.)

    a.   many years of drought

    b.   rain patterns

    c.   man's use of the land

    d.   huge sandstorms covering the topsoil with sand over hundreds of years

3. Which sentence from the passage would support the model statement?

    Model: Even today, the forests of the world are shrinking.

    _____

    _____

4. Which of the following is an *opinion?*

    a.   Desert land is best used for something productive such as farming.

    b.   In order to grow crops in the desert, they need to be irrigated.

    c.   Many forms of wildlife would die out if deserts were destroyed.

    d.   The Sahara is the largest desert in the world.

5. All of the following were mentioned in the passage as man's use of land that may cause the development of a desert **except**:

    a.   overgrazing of livestock

    b.   extended plowing of the land

    c.   cutting down forests

    d.   planting crops that need large amounts of water

6. Choose the best possible meaning for the underlined word in the model sentence.

   Model: The loss of topsoil resulted in a <u>reduction</u> of plants that could grow.

   a. variety

   b. decrease

   c. rare type

   d. surprising number

7. According to the passage, which of the following do rainforests and deserts have in common?

   a. They both have a wide variety of animals.

   b. One has lots of rain and the other one doesn't.

   c. Each area is disappearing at the same rate.

   d. One is man-made and the other one isn't.

8. When *comparing* deserts with rainforests, which of the following cognitive maps would probably work best?

   a. B

   b. C

   c. D

   d. A

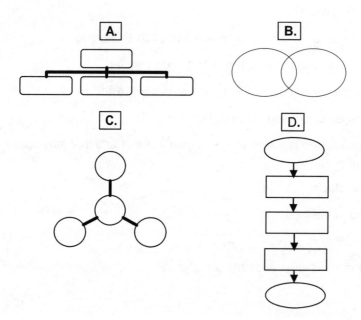

Part E - Bonus Review

Here is an **idiom**: "know the ropes." When you belong to any organization, such as scouts, or a club, or even your school, you need to know the rules of the organization and how things work there.

Sailors of sailing vessels literally need to know the ropes. That is, they need to know which rope controls which sail on the boat.

Read this **quatrain stanza** from a Longfellow poem:

> The first slight swerving of the heart,
>
> That words are powerless to express,
>
> And leave it still unsaid in part,
>
> Or say it in too great excess.

The **rhyming pattern** of this **stanza** is: a b a b.

Each one of the four lines is **quatrameter**. Each line has four **metrical feet**.

Lesson 48

Part A - Poetry

Directions: After you read stanzas 5 through 9 of "The Raven," answer the questions. You may look at Part A of Lesson 47 to help you answer the questions.

Stanza 5

Deep into that darkness peering, long I stood there wondering, fearing,

Doubting, dreaming dreams no mortal ever dared to dream to dream before

But the silence was unbroken, and the darkness gave no token,

And the only word there spoken was the whispered word, `Lenore!'

This I whispered, and an echo murmured back the word, `Lenore!'

Merely this and nothing more.

Stanza 6

Back into the chamber turning, all my soul within me burning,

Soon again I heard a tapping somewhat louder than before.

`Surely,' said I, `surely that is something at my window lattice;

Let me see then, what the threat is, and this mystery explore -

Let my heart be still a moment and this mystery explore; -

'Tis the wind and nothing more!'

Stanza 7

Open here I flung the shutter, when, with many a flirt and flutter,

In there stepped a stately raven of the saintly days of yore.

Not the least obeisance made he; not an instant stopped or stayed he;

But, with mien of lord or lady, perched above my chamber door -

Perched upon a bust of Pallas just above my chamber door -

Perched, and sat, and nothing more.

Stanza 8

Then this ebony bird beguiling my sad fancy into smiling,

By the grave and stern decorum of the countenance it wore,

`Though thy crest be shorn and shaven, thou,' I said, `art sure no craven.

Ghastly grim and ancient raven wandering from the nightly shore -

Tell me what thy lordly name is on the Night's Plutonian shore!'

Quoth the raven, `Nevermore.'

Stanza 9

Much I marveled this ungainly fowl to hear discourse so plainly,

Though its answer little meaning - little relevancy bore;

For we cannot help agreeing that no living human being

Ever yet was blessed with seeing bird above his chamber door -

Bird or beast above the sculptured bust above his chamber door,

With such name as `Nevermore.'

1. What do the first and third lines of all these stanzas have in common?

    _____

2. What do the first five lines of all the stanzas have in common?

    _____

3. What do the sixth lines of all the stanzas have in common?

    _____

4. Which words in the ninth stanza are internal rhymes?

    _____

5. These stanzas all have six lines. What do we call a stanza with six lines?

    _____

Part B - Paraphrase Paragraph

Directions: Paraphrase the paragraph below. The paragraph structure is provided for you in the chart below the paragraph. Write about the parts of the paragraph structure, using your own words.

The same drops of water on Earth that were created billions of years ago are still being used. They continuously move from the oceans, to the air, to the land, and back to the oceans again. The sun's heat evaporates water from the oceans. The water rises as invisible vapor, or gas, and falls back to Earth as moisture. This moisture is called *precipitation*. Precipitation develops when water vapor in the atmosphere condenses into clouds, and some form of moisture falls to the earth, such as rain or snow. Most precipitation drops back directly into the oceans. The remainder falls on the rest of the Earth. In time, this water also returns to the sea, and the cycle starts again. This unending circulation of the Earth's waters is called the *water cycle*.

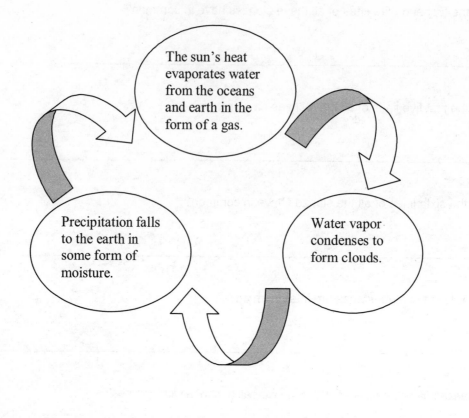

The sun's heat evaporates water from the oceans and earth in the form of a gas.

Water vapor condenses to form clouds.

Precipitation falls to the earth in some form of moisture.

_____

_____

_____

_____

_____

Part C - Review

Directions: Read the flyer below and then answer the questions.

Apartments for Rent
Available October 1ˢᵗ

- Rent ranging from $500 to $1,000 per month
- $500 deposit required plus first and last month's rent
- One, two, and three bedrooms available
- 1 ½ or 2 bathroom units (depending on size)
- **Small** pets allowed. Extra $200 deposit required for dogs up to 50 lbs
- Close to schools, parks, churches, and hospitals
- Water, sewer, and garbage included
- Furnished and unfurnished units available
- Range, refrigerator, microwave, washer and dryer included
- Some covered parking available for an additional fee

Two locations! Westside near freeway entrance AND
Downtown near state office buildings

Contact person: Nancy Marconi, Manager
Phone: 555-1212

| Nancy Marconi 555-1212 | Nancy Marconi 555-1212 | Nancy Marconi 555-1212 | Nancy Marconi 555-1212 | Nancy Marconi 555-1212 | Nancy Marconi 555-1212 |

1. You would most likely find an advertisement of this type in:

    a.   the daily newspaper

    b.   bulletin board at the grocery store

    c.   tourist magazine

    d.   internet

2. Which of the following amount of rent would you **not** be expected to pay for one of these apartments?

    a. $700.00 per month

    b. $1,000.00 per month

    c. $456.00 per month

    d. $645.00 per month

3. Explain a possible reason for the name and number of the manager to be repeated at the bottom of the advertisement.

_____

_____

4. Which of the following is **not** an option when renting one of these apartments?

    a.   washer and dryer

    b.   covered parking

    c.   number of bedrooms

    d.   furnished or unfurnished

5. What important piece of information is missing from this advertisement?

    a.   the locations of the apartments

    b.   amount of deposit

    c.   the rules about pets

    d.   the name of the apartment complex

6. In this advertisement, the word *ranging* means:

    a.   varying

    b.   extending

    c.   changing

    d.   continuing

Part F - Bonus Review

These words describe the number of **metrical feet** in a line of poetry.

quatrameter: four metrical feet

pentameter: five metrical feet

octameter: eight metrical feet

Read this **quatrain stanza** from a Longfellow poem:

>The first slight swerving of the heart,
>
>That words are powerless to express,
>
>And leave it still unsaid in part,
>
>Or say it in too great excess.

The **rhyming pattern** is: a b a b.

Anaphora means "a pronoun or other words used to refer to some other word or name."

The two words in bold below are anaphora referring to "The Chicago Cubs."

>My neighbor loves the Chicago Cubs. He bought a special satellite package just so he could watch all the **Cubbies** games from his home in Arizona. Every year, he thinks **they** will go to the World Series.

Lesson 49

Part A - Poetry

Directions: After you quickly review stanzas 10 through 18 of "The Raven," follow the directions.

<u>Stanza 10</u>

But the raven, sitting lonely on the placid bust, spoke only,

That one word, as if his soul in that one word he did outpour.

Nothing further then he uttered - not a feather then he fluttered -

Till I scarcely more than muttered `Other friends have flown before -

On the morrow will he leave me, as my hopes have flown before.'

Then the bird said, `Nevermore.'

<u>Stanza 11</u>

Startled at the stillness broken by reply so aptly spoken,

`Doubtless,' said I, `what it utters is its only stock and store,

Caught from some unhappy master whom unmerciful disaster

Followed fast and followed faster till his songs one burden bore -

Till the dirges of his hope that melancholy burden bore

Of "Never-nevermore."'

Stanza 12

But the raven still beguiling all my sad soul into smiling,

Straight I wheeled a cushioned seat in front of bird and bust and door;

Then, upon the velvet sinking, I betook myself to linking

Fancy unto fancy, thinking what this ominous bird of yore -

What this grim, ungainly, gaunt, and ominous bird of yore

Meant in croaking `Nevermore.'

Stanza 13

This I sat engaged in guessing, but no syllable expressing

To the fowl whose fiery eyes now burned into my bosom's core;

This and more I sat divining, with my head at ease reclining

On the cushion's velvet violet lining that the lamp-light gloated o'er,

But whose velvet violet lining with the lamp-light gloating o'er,

She shall press, ah, nevermore!

Stanza 14

Then, methought, the air grew denser, perfumed from an unseen censer

Swung by angels whose faint foot-falls tinkled on the tufted floor.

`Wretch,' I cried, `thy God hath lent thee - by these angels he has sent thee

Respite - respite and nepenthe from the memories of Lenore!

Quaff, oh quaff this kind nepenthe, and forget this lost Lenore!'

Quoth the raven, `Nevermore.'

Stanza 15

`Prophet!' said I, `thing of evil! - prophet still, if bird or devil! -

Whether tempter sent, or whether tempest tossed thee here ashore,

Desolate yet all undaunted, on this desert land enchanted -

On this home by horror haunted - tell me truly, I implore -

Is there - is there balm in Gilead? - tell me - tell me, I implore!'

Quoth the raven, `Nevermore.'

Stanza 16

`Prophet!' said I, `thing of evil! - prophet still, if bird or devil!

By that Heaven that bends above us - by that God we both adore -

Tell this soul with sorrow laden if, within the distant Aidenn,

It shall clasp a sainted maiden whom the angels named Lenore -

Clasp a rare and radiant maiden, whom the angels named Lenore?'

Quoth the raven, `Nevermore.'

Stanza 17

`Be that word our sign of parting, bird or fiend!' I shrieked upstarting -

`Get thee back into the tempest and the Night's Plutonian shore!

Leave no black plume as a token of that lie thy soul hath spoken!

Leave my loneliness unbroken! - quit the bust above my door!

Take thy beak from out my heart, and take thy form from off my door!'

Quoth the raven, `Nevermore.'

Stanza 18

And the raven, never flitting, still is sitting, still is sitting

On the pallid bust of Pallas just above my chamber door;

And his eyes have all the seeming of a demon's that is dreaming,

And the lamp-light o'er him streaming throws his shadow on the floor;

And my soul from out that shadow that lies floating on the floor

Shall be lifted - nevermore!

Write a brief analysis of the following elements of the last nine stanzas: metrical feet, number of lines per stanza, and internal rhyme.

_____

_____

_____

_____

Part B - Paraphrase Paragraph

Directions: Paraphrase the paragraph below. The paragraph structure is provided for you. Write about the parts of the paragraph structure using your own words.

I have never really liked writing stories or reports. Don't get me wrong. I liked learning the information, but I could never see why I had to write it all down on paper. I always waited until the night before the paper was due to sit down and start writing it. I'd begin by writing down everything I could remember reading about the subject I was reporting on. If it was a story, I'd just write down anything that popped into my head. When my teacher returned my paper, I was always shocked. There were more red circles, check marks, question marks, and lines drawn through sentences than you could shake a stick at. I did so poorly, my parents had to sign the papers and I was required to do them over. Because I was doing most of the papers twice, I was always behind. Finally, I stayed after school and asked for a little extra help from my teacher. I learned how to organize my thoughts before I ever began to write. I also used a dictionary and a thesaurus. When I had finished writing a paper, I would proofread it carefully and correct my spelling mistakes. I also changed sentences that were incomplete, run-ons, or were unclear. I was a pretty poor student in writing until I took the time to learn a few good study skills.

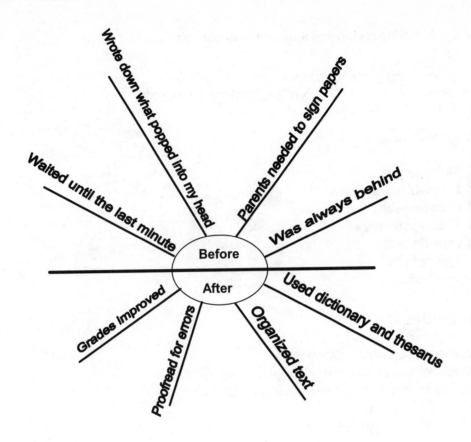

Before

After

Wrote down what popped into my head

Parents needed to sign papers

Waited until the last minute

Was always behind

Grades improved

Used dictionary and thesarus

Proofread for errors

Organized text

Part C - Review

Directions: Read the following recipe and answer the questions.

Soft Chewy Pretzels

Ingredients:

1 package yeast
1 1/2 cups warm water
1 teaspoon salt
1 Tablespoon sugar
4 cups flour
1 egg, beaten
coarse salt

Directions:

Preheat the oven to 425 degrees.
Measure warm water into large mixing bowl.
Sprinkle on yeast and stir until it looks soft.
Add salt, sugar and flour.
Mix and knead dough.

Take a small ball of dough to roll or twist into pretzels, letters, numerals or other interesting shapes.
Grease cookie sheets.
Lay twisted shapes on cookie sheets.
*Brush dough with beaten egg and sprinkle with coarse salt.
Bake at 425 degrees for 12 to 15 minutes.

* Variations:
Try sprinkling dough with grated cheese before baking.
Dip baked shapes in melted butter and sprinkle with cinnamon and sugar.

1. You would most likely be able to find this recipe in each of the following **except**:

    a. a children's cookbook

    b. a science book with experiments

    c. a monthly home magazine

    d. a lawn and garden magazine

2. Which of the following statements is a **fact** that can be supported by information in the recipe?

    a. This dough works best when shaped as a pretzel.

    b. This dough can be made into many different shapes before baking.

    c. Salt is the only topping you can put on the dough.

    d. Yeast is the most important ingredient in this recipe.

3. Circle the sentence from the recipe that supports your choice in question number two.

4. The purpose of this type of passage is to help someone:

    a. tell a story

    b. follow directions in order to make something

    c. to think in a certain way

    d. organize information

5. Which ingredients are mixed together *first*?

    a. sugar and cinnamon

    b. salt, sugar, and flour

    c. yeast and sugar

    d. water and yeast

6. Which word in the recipe indicates that there are different toppings and additions you can try when making this recipe?

    a. knead

    b. variations

    c. preheat

    d. coarse

7. What might happen after someone makes this recipe once if they like the way the pretzels come out?

_____

_____

Part D - Bonus Review

A **stanza** of a poem with four lines is called a **quatrain**.

A **stanza** of a poem with six lines is called a **sestet**.

An **internal rhyme** is a word within a line that rhymes with another word at the end of the line.

Here is part of a poem by Paul Lawrence Dunbar. The two **stanzas** shown are **quatrain**. The **rhyming pattern** is: a b c b.

So it pushed a little leaflet

Up into the light of day,

To examine the surroundings

And show the rest the way.

The leaflet liked the prospect,

So it called its brother, Stem;

Then two other leaflets heard it,

And quickly followed them.

Lesson 51

Part A - Author's Purpose

You know that authors have different purposes for writing the things they write. Good authors also have reasons for each *part* of something they write.

In the passage below from Lesson 36, the author has a purpose for the first paragraph. To figure out why that part is in the passage, think about what the passage would be like without it. Without the first introductory paragraph, the passage would start right out talking about safety pins, and that might not be as interesting.

The author is trying to get the reader interested in the introduction by asking questions in the form of a riddle.

It's shiny, it's safe, and it can hold things together, as well as being multi-useful. How many times have you heard someone ask the question, "Does anyone have a _____? It's an emergency!" The words most likely used to fill in the bank are "safety pin."

The safety pin is the invention of a mechanic from New York named Walter Hunt. Walter Hunt also built America's first sewing machine. He later lost interest in patenting his sewing machine because he believed the invention would cause a rise in unemployment. The safety pin was invented while Walter Hunt was twisting a piece of wire, trying to think of something that would help him pay off a fifteen dollar debt. On April 10, 1849, the safety pin was patented.

Walter Hunt didn't think much of his safety pin as an invention, so he soon sold the patent for four hundred dollars. Then, he watched as the buyer became a millionaire!

Part B - Author's Purpose

Directions: Read the passage in Part A about safety pins again. Next, answer the questions.

1. To figure out why the author wrote the second paragraph of the passage, think about what the passage would be like *without* that paragraph. Would you know what else Walter Hunt had invented if the second paragraph was not included?

_____

2. Why would the author include the reason Walter Hunt didn't patent his invention of the sewing machine?

_____

_____

Part C - Paraphrase Paragraph

Directions: Paraphrase the paragraphs below. Part of the paragraph structure is provided for you. Provide the additional information needed in the paragraph structure. Then, write a paraphrase of the paragraph, using your own words.

A tapestry is textile that is hand woven. The weaving of textiles by hand demands a lot of time and a great deal of skill. Other artists either have a canvas to paint, clay to model, or wood or stone to carve. Using only heavy colored threads, a weaver must assemble and decorate his textile at the same time. Artists who are patient, able to plan ahead, and have the skill to weave are one in a million, so tapestries are very expensive treasures. Most tapestries are hung on walls or from ceilings.

Historically, tapestries were seen as symbols of wealth. Tapestries were used to add beauty and richness to plays, official ceremonies, or public celebrations. Bishops and kings welcomed important visitors with red carpets flanked by tapestry displays.

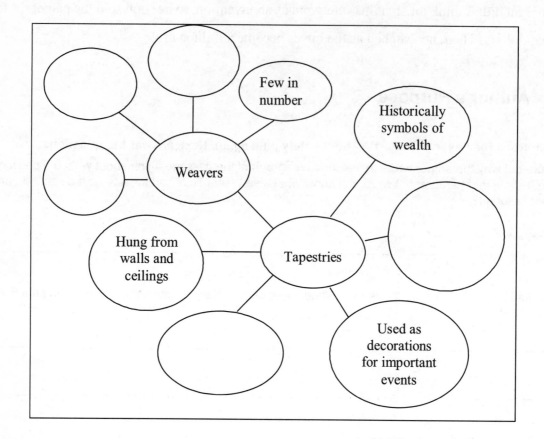

_____

_____

_____

_____

_____

Part D - Review

Directions: Read the flyer below and answer the questions.

"Loved to Death" Sneaker Contest
Saturday, June 14th, 2:00pm
Just Right Shoe Store

Qualifications:
- Must be between the ages of 5 & 15.
- Have a pair of revolting old sneakers.

Scoring:
Points will be awarding in the following categories :

Must smell rotten	Frayed laces
Torn seams	Worn soles
Holes	Sagging tongues

* Shoes must be in good enough condition to be worn.

* Local winner will be automatically be entered in the National Contest in Lawrence, Kansas, July 7th.

* All expenses for 4 to the National Contest will be paid.

* Winner of the national contest receives a trophy, $100 and a new pair of tennis shoes!

In order to enter this contest, just fill out the form below and drop it in the mail or drop it by the store. It's as easy as tying your shoelaces or buckling your Velcro!

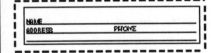

NAME
ADDRESS   PHONE

Mail to:

Loved to Death Sneaker Contest
c/o Just Right Shoe Store
3725 Lakeside Drive
Sunnyvale, Washington 98501

Lesson 51

1. What information in this ad would most likely get people to enter the contest?

    a.   winning a new pair of tennis shoes

    b.   being entered into the national contest

    c.   receiving $100

    d.   being awarded a trophy

2. All of these are required on the entry form **except**:

    a.   address

    b.   name

    c.   parent signature

    d.   phone

3. The word "revolting" is used in this ad to mean:

    a.   disgusting

    b.   stylish

    c.   expensive

    d.   colorful

4. Explain why this contest is called the "Loved to Death" sneaker contest.

    _____

    _____

    _____

5. To enter this contest you must be between the ages of:

    a.   10 and 15

    b.   5 and 10

    c.   5 and 15

    d.   15 and 20

6. This contest is probably held in order to:

    a.   bring people into the store hoping they'll look around and perhaps buy a pair of shoes

    b.   give the young people of the town something to look forward to

    c.   help bring tourists to Kansas.

    d.   get rid of some extra shoes that aren't selling

7. What is one requirement in order to win?

    a.   The shoes must use velcro.

    b.   You must have 3 other people willing to go to Lawrence, Kansas with you.

    c.   You must have bought a pair of shoes at the store within the last year.

    d.   The shoes must be in good enough condition to wear.

8. The "c/o" in the mailing address most likely means:

    a.   the abbreviation for the state of Colorado

    b.   care of

    c.   come on in

    d.   construction over

Part E - Bonus

A **myth** is a traditional or legendary story. The stories are usually about heroic human beings and the various gods people believed in long ago. **Mythology** is the study of **myths**. The authors of many books and poems often refer to characters from **mythology**. For example, Edgar Allen Poe refers to "Pallas" in "The Raven." Pallas was a goddess of wisdom in Greek **mythology**. **Myth** comes from a Greek word meaning "story."

BONUS REVIEW
Quatrain and **sestet** refer to the number of lines in a **stanza**. A **quatrain** has four lines and a **sestet** has six. **Quatrameter** refers to the number of **metrical feet** in a poem. A **trochee** is a type of **metrical foot**.

Lesson 52

Part A - Author's Purpose

Directions: Read the passage below from Lesson 36 and then answer the questions.

It's shiny, it's safe, and it can hold things together, as well as being multi-useful. How many times have you heard someone ask the question, "Does anyone have a _____? It's an emergency!" The words most likely used to fill in the bank are "safety pin."

The safety pin is the invention of a mechanic from New York named Walter Hunt. Walter Hunt also built America's first sewing machine. He later lost interest in patenting his sewing machine because he believed the invention would cause a rise in unemployment. The safety pin was invented while Walter Hunt was twisting a piece of wire, trying to think of something that would help him pay off a fifteen dollar debt. On April 10, 1849, the safety pin was patented. Walter Hunt didn't think much of his safety pin as an invention, so he soon sold the patent for four hundred dollars. Then, he watched as that person proceeded to become a millionaire!

1. Why did the author use a common situation in the opening paragraph?

_____

_____

2. Why would the author want you to have the information about *why* Walter Hunt invented the safety pin?

_____

_____

Part B- Paraphrase Paragraph

Directions: Paraphrase the paragraphs below. Part of the paragraph structure is provided for you. Provide the additional information needed in the paragraph structure. Then, write a paraphrase of the paragraphs, using your own words.

A fossil hunter's dream came true when, in November 1998, American and local scientists, on an expedition in an out-of-the-way part of Argentina, stumbled on a dinosaur nesting site. The site was cluttered with pieces of fossilized dinosaur eggs the size of grapefruits. For the first time, fossil remains of unhatched dinosaurs were among the eggs. Some were preserved so well that even the scales on their skin could be seen. Besides fossilized skin, the scientists found teeth and bones of unhatched dinosaurs.

There were thousands of eggs at the Argentinean site laid by dinosaurs called titanosaurs. They probably nested there year after year. They laid their eggs near streams. Sometimes the streams flooded, covering the eggs with mud before they could hatch. Over millions of years, the mud turned to stone, and the buried eggs turned into fossils.

Who?	What?	When?	Where?	Why?
	Found dinosaur nesting places with many eggs		Out of the way place in Argentina	Eggs laid near stream

Pieces of fossil eggs

↓

Remains of unhatched dinosaurs

↓

[ ]

Eggs turned to

_____

_____

_____

_____

_____

Part C - Review

Directions: Read the passage and answer the questions.

The Sahara Desert covers 3,500,000 miles or about 25% of Africa! It is the largest desert in the world. The name *Sahara* is an English pronunciation of the Arabic word for desert.

In the Sahara you will find mountains, rocky areas, gravel plains, salt flats, and huge areas of dunes. Some places in the central Sahara sometimes get no rain for years at a time. There are fewer than 2 million people who call the Sahara Desert home. Most of these people are Arabic nomads. Nomads are people that have no permanent home. They constantly travel in search of food and water for themselves, their families, and their animals.

The Sahara has been crossed by Arab caravans looking for gold, ivory, grain, salt and slaves since the 10th century. But much has changed since those days. Many of the native Arabs have moved to Saharan cities like Cairo, Egypt, Africa's largest city. Camels have been replaced by trucks in the salt trade. Many Tuaregs, a people native to the Sahara, make their living acting as guides to tourists. And oil and gas operations stand to bring far greater wealth to the area and its people than gold and ivory ever could.

There are <u>prehistoric</u> rock paintings in Algeria that show that giraffes, elephants, and lions once lived in the Sahara. Today, the only animals you'll find there are the ones that can survive the scorching heat and <u>utter</u> lack of water. Rodents, snakes and scorpions rule the desert. During the day, the temperature reaches about 109 degrees on average but at night, it can fall below freezing.

1. Which of the following titles BEST tells what this story is about?

    a. All About the World's Largest Desert

    b. Animals of the Sahara

    c. Cairo, Africa's Largest City

    d. Algerian Rock Paintings

2. Which of the following statements is a fact supported by information in the passage?

    a. The Sahara Desert is very sparsely populated.

    b. Cairo, Egypt has many tourist attractions.

    c. It is better to work as a guide for tourists than to sell gold.

    d. Gold and ivory jewelry are very popular in Africa.

3. Which one of the following words, and its definition, would best match the underlined word in the model sentence?

    Model: There are <u>prehistoric</u> rock paintings in Algeria that show that giraffes, elephants, and lions once lived in the Sahara.

    a. pretty; attractive

    b. traditional; customary

    c. professional; skillful

    d. ancient; from the time before written history

4. Which one of the following phrases lets the reader know that the Sahara is a more modern place than it once was?

    a. . . . you will find mountains, rocky areas . . .

    b. They constantly travel . . .

    c. Camels have been replaced by trucks. . .

    d. The Sahara has been crossed by Arab caravans . . .

5. Choose the sentence that uses the underlined word in the same way as the model sentence.

    Model: Rodents, snakes and scorpions <u>rule</u> the desert.

    a. One <u>rule</u> we follow in school is: always raise your hand before speaking.

    b. I think the judge will <u>rule</u> in Jason's favor.

    c. As a <u>rule</u>, I don't enjoy eating fish.

    d. The winner of the spelling bee <u>ruled</u> the stage as she took her bows.

6. Which of the following definitions best fits the underlined word, <u>utter</u>, in the last paragraph?

    a. terrible

    b. total

    c. terrific

    d. tranquil

7. What new industries promise to bring great wealth to the Sahara and its people:

    a. farming and ranching

    b. grain and salt

    c. oil and gas

    d. gold and ivory

Part D - Bonus

Mythology is the study of **myths**. A **myth** is a story with heroic characters and gods called "deities," such as Pallas, the goddess of wisdom. To understand what you are reading, you sometimes have to know about some **mythological** characters.

BONUS REVIEW

Here is an **idiom**: "tempest in a teapot." A tempest is a big storm, but the storm couldn't be very big if it was inside of a teapot. When we say that something is a tempest in a teapot, we mean that thing causes a lot of excitement, but isn't actually very important. When baseball players throw a big fit over an umpire's call, that is usually a tempest in a teapot.

Lesson 53

Part A - Author's Purpose

Directions: Read the passage below from Lesson 51 and then answer the questions.

A tapestry is textile that is hand woven. The weaving of textiles by hand demands a lot of time and a great deal of skill. Other artists either have a canvas to paint, clay to model, or wood or stone to carve. Using only heavy colored threads, a weaver must assemble and decorate his textile at the same time. Artists who are patient, able to plan ahead, and have the skill to weave are one in a million, so tapestries are very expensive treasures. Most tapestries are hung on walls or from ceilings.

Historically, tapestries were seen as symbols of wealth. Tapestries were used to add beauty and richness to plays, official ceremonies, or public celebrations. Bishops and kings welcomed important visitors with red carpets flanked by tapestry displays.

1. What would you not know if the last paragraph was not in the passage?

_____

_____

2. Why would the author want you to have the information about weavers in the first paragraph?

_____

_____

Part B - Paraphrase Paragraph

Directions: Paraphrase the paragraphs below. Part of the paragraph structure is provided for you. Provide the additional information needed in the paragraph structure. Then, write a paraphrase of the paragraphs, using your own words.

If you look at any mathematics book written shortly before the 1500's, it will be very hard to understand. Although we may recognize the numerals that we use now, everything else was different then. The signs and symbols that we know and use when we study mathematics now had not yet been invented then.

The familiar (+) sign for addition and the (-) sign for subtraction first appeared in 1489 in a German arithmetic book. The book was never published, however. They may have been borrowed from signs used by merchants to mark certain packages. A (+) was marked on packages with too much of whatever the package contained, while a (-) meant too little.

The (=) sign for "equals" was invented in 1557 by an English mathematician. Another Englishman invented the (x) sign for multiplication in 1631. The (÷) sign for division was actually invented earlier by a German mathematician, but did not appear in a mathematics book until 1659.

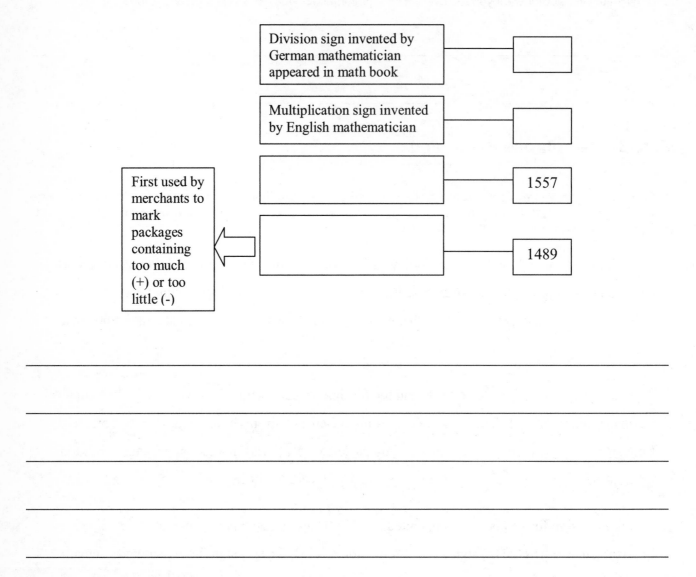

Part C - Review

Directions: Read the passage and then answer the questions.

It is a wondrous thing to look up at the stars at night. They have inspired painters, authors, poets. We cast our eyes to the sky and send our fondest wishes up to the stars hoping they will come true. But have you ever wondered, as you make your wishes, which stars you're wishing upon? You could be wishing upon Vega, Sirius, Castor or Polaris. With thousands and thousands of stars in the sky, people needed a way to keep track of them all. And so they came up with the constellations.

Constellations are actually 88 separate areas into which astronomers have divided the sky. But we usually use the word constellation to refer to a grouping of stars that seem to form a picture or pattern in the sky.

While we're not certain, many historians believe the naming of constellations began around 6,000 years ago. Constellations served a very important purpose. Different groups of stars are visible at different times of the year which means you can use the constellations to tell what month it is. Farmers could tell by what constellations were visible in the sky whether it was Spring or Fall and therefore whether it was time to <u>plant</u> their crops or harvest them.

Many of the Constellations' names come from the ancient Greeks. They used to name the star patterns after their Gods, heroes and mythological characters. Some other names come from the ancient Romans. While there are 88 official constellations, some are more well known than others. Some that you might recognize are Gemini, Libra, Leo and Sagitarius. However, the most famous constellation isn't a constellation at all! The Big Dipper is really an asterism, which is an identifiable shape formed by stars that is actually only part of a constellation. The asterism The Big Dipper is really part of the constellation Ursa Major which means "Great Bear" in Latin. The Big Dipper is made of the seven brightest stars in Ursa Major; those seven stars make up the hindquarters and tail of the Great Bear.

1. This story is mostly about:

    a. The Big Dipper

    b. how farmers know when to plant crops

    c. what the constellations are and how and why people started naming them

    d. ancient Greek mythology

2. A person viewing The Big Dipper for the first time would probably experience a feeling of:

    a. fear

    b. frustration

    c. amazement

    d. disappointment

3. Which of the following is the best summary statement for paragraph number 3?

    a.   When constellations were first named, they were very important for helping farmers know when to plant and harvest crops.

    b.   Constellations were first named about 6,000 years ago.

    c.   Certain constellations are only visible in the Spring.

    d.   Constellations are still important today.

4. Choose the sentence that uses the underlined word in the same way as the model sentence.

Model: Farmers could tell by what constellations were visible in the sky whether it was Spring or Fall and therefore whether it was time to <u>plant</u> their crops or harvest them.

    a.   The big fern in our living room is my mom's favorite <u>plant</u>.

    b.   When I was learning how to golf, my instructor told me I had to <u>plant</u> my feet.

    c.   There is a paper manufacturing <u>plant</u> that employs many people who live in the town.

    d.   My favorite thing to do is <u>plant</u> bulbs in the Fall.

5. Briefly explain what the first and fourth paragraphs have in common.

_____

_____

6. The Big Dipper is:

    a.   a constellation

    b.   an asterism

    c.   the Great Bear

    d.   a star

Part D - Bonus

A **myth** is a story with heroic characters and deities, such as Pallas, the goddess of wisdom. You have probably heard of some **mythological** deities, such as Venus, the goddess of love.

BONUS REVIEW

This is a **cognitive map**. It shows the organization of ideas.

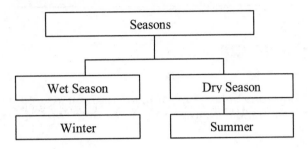

Lesson 54

Part A - Author's Purpose

Directions: Read the passage below from Lesson 51 and then answer the questions.

A tapestry is textile that is hand woven. The weaving of textiles by hand demands a lot of time and a great deal of skill. Other artists either have a canvas to paint, clay to model, or wood or stone to carve. Using only heavy colored threads, a weaver must assemble and decorate his textile at the same time. Artists who are patient, able to plan ahead, and have the skill to weave are one in a million, so tapestries are very expensive treasures. Most tapestries are hung on walls or from ceilings.

Historically, tapestries were seen as symbols of wealth. Tapestries were used to add beauty and richness to plays, official ceremonies, or public celebrations. Bishops and kings welcomed important visitors with red carpets flanked by tapestry displays.

1. What phrase does the author use in the first paragraph to show the reader that there are only a few people who have the skills necessary to be good weavers?

---

2. Instead of asking a question, what did the author use to begin the first paragraph?

Part B - Paraphrase Paragraph

Directions: Paraphrase the paragraphs below. Part of the paragraph structure is provided for you. Provide the additional information needed in the paragraph structure. Then, write a paraphrase of the paragraphs, using your own words.

Mythologists are interested in the fact that myths are found almost everywhere in the world. However, they don't agree on how myths become so widely spread. One theory is that stories created in early times spread when the communities that began the stories broke into separate groups. Those groups migrated to different parts of the world, and their stories went with them.

A second theory is that myths were passed back and forth between neighboring societies and carried along trade routes. They were traded in the same way that merchandise and ideas have long been exchanged among different populations.

Other mythologists present a third theory. They argue that all people, no matter where they live, share some common experiences and react to these experiences in similar ways. It is only natural that people in different parts of the world would have similar stories to explain the origin of the world and the nature of the various things within it.

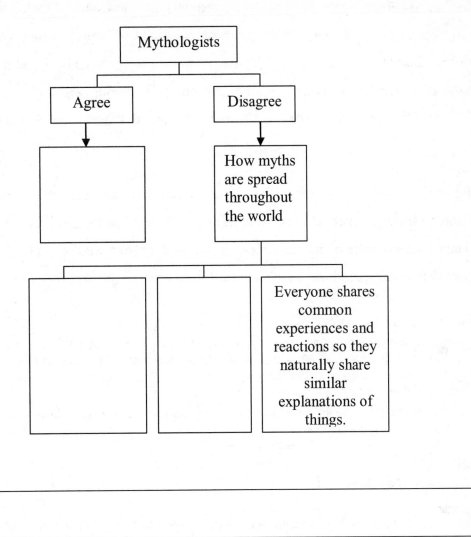

Part C - Review

Directions: Read the passage and then answer the questions.

On Tuesday, I thought I was going to be in the worst trouble I had ever been in. Some friends and I were playing catch in my front yard after school. We were kind of goofing around, trying to throw the ball as hard as we could. If the ball is thrown hard enough and it hits right in the pocket of the glove, you can hear a "pop." When you hear that sound, it's a pretty safe bet the hand inside that glove is stinging just a little bit. Well, when I had the ball, I reared back and let it fly. Unfortunately, it sailed over everyone's heads and smashed into our neighbor's window. I have never seen my "friends" run so fast! I was scared to death, but I knew what had to be done, so I did it.

I didn't say anything to my parents about the window because I didn't want to get grounded. That would mean I'd be unable to play in the game on Saturday. I figured I'd tell them after the game. The next night though, my parents came into my room and wanted me to read a letter they had gotten in the mail. Here's what the letter said:

> Dear Mr. and Mrs. Robertson,
>
> I'm enclosing a bill for replacing my living room window. Your son, Peter, came to my door and admitted he was the one who threw the ball that broke the widow. The other children scattered when it happened, but Peter came to my door and offered to pay for the broken window out of his allowance and his paper route money.
>
> You are both to be praised for establishing such a strong sense of responsibility in your son. Please show him the bill is marked "PAID" because I was so impressed with his honesty. However, I do hope he will be more careful in the future.
>
> Sincerely,
>
> Mrs. Howe

Whew, was I relieved. My parents weren't mad at all, but they did tell me that the next time anything like that happened to be sure to tell them right away. The first night after it happened, I didn't sleep very well. I'm sure tonight is going to be a different story.

1. The author of this passage is:

   a. Mrs. Howe

   b. Peter

   c. one of Peter's friends

   d. Peter's parents

2. Which of the following phrases best applies to this passage?

    a. He who laughs last laughs best.

    b. Money is the root of all evil.

    c. Truth is stranger than fiction.

    d. Honesty is the best policy.

3. The author put the word "friends" in quotation marks to show that:

    a. there were too many to list all the names, so he just referred to them as "friends"

    b. they weren't really such good friends because they all ran away and left him alone

    c. he didn't know all of their names

    d. they weren't really his friends, just some kids in the neighborhood

4. Peter and his parents impressed Mrs. Howe because:

    a. they keep their lawn neat and tidy

    b. they check on her often to see if she needs anything

    c. they taught Peter responsibility, and he followed through when he made a mistake

    d. they make sure Peter and his friends aren't too loud when playing in the front yard

5. Which of the following best describes Mrs. Howe?

    a. disappointed

    b. mean

    c. unfair

    d. generous

6. Which words in the passage tell the reader that Peter is responsible?

    a. I didn't say anything to my parents about the window because I didn't want to get grounded...

    b. ...I knew what had to be done, so I did it.

    c. I figured I'd tell them after the game.

    d. ...I didn't sleep very well.

7. Choose the best possible meaning for the underlined word in the model sentence.
Model: You are both to be praised for instilling such a strong <u>sense</u> of responsibility in your son.

    a. a function of the body such as sight, taste, or touch

    b. ability

    c. awareness

    d. good reason or excuse

Part D - Bonus

A **myth** is a story with heroic characters and deities, such as Venus, the goddess of love. To understand what you are reading, you sometimes have to know about some **mythological** characters.

BONUS REVIEW

Here is part of a poem by Robert Frost. The **rhyming pattern** is: a b a a b.

> And both that morning equally lay
>
> In leaves no step had trodden black.
>
> Oh, I kept the first for another day!
>
> Yet knowing how way leads on to way,
>
> I doubted if I should ever come back.

An **internal rhyme** is a word within a line that rhymes with another word at the end of the line. Words that end with similar—but not exactly the same—sounds are **partial rhymes**.

Lesson 56

Part A - Author's Purpose

Directions: Read the passage below and answer the questions.

Realistic art is just what the words suggest. It's realistic. If no one ever told you what a specific realistic painting was about, it would be easy to imagine the story behind the painting just by looking at it. A famous painting called *The Banjo Lesson* is an example of realistic art.

In this famous painting, a young boy is sitting on a man's knee, holding a banjo. Their heads are close together and they are both looking at the banjo. By looking at the expression on their faces, there is a feeling that the boy is getting encouragement from the man. Just by looking at the details of the picture it is quite clear that the boy and the man have a close relationship and they both share the experience of playing the banjo.

The artist who painted *The Banjo Lesson* is an African-American by the name of Henry O. Tanner. Although Tanner went to one of the finest art schools in the United States, he found it difficult to make a living by painting. Unfortunately, African-Americans were still not accepted as equals in the 1890s, even though slavery had ended decades earlier. Finally, Tanner decided to leave the United States and live and study in Paris. *The Banjo Lesson* was painted shortly after he arrived there.

Tanner and other realistic artists tried hard to make their paintings very true to life. Soon though, artists began to leave realism and look at new ways of representing the world on canvas. Monet painted his "impressions" of what he saw instead of a detailed image. Vincent van Gogh wanted to show what his eyes saw, but also what his heart and his mind felt.

1. What would you probably be able to do after reading the first paragraph?

_____

_____

2. What do you think the author would like you to remember most from the third paragraph?

_____

_____

Part B- Paraphrase Paragraph

Directions: Read the paragraph below. Write the details from the paragraph in the list below. Then, write a paraphrase of the paragraph using your own words.

Ancient Greece was made up of independent city-states. Each city-state was called a "polis." Each polis was made up of a city and the lands surrounding it. Each one had its own government and operated almost like a small country. The people living in each polis had to obey its leaders and its laws. City-states constantly competed with each other for power and glory. They competed through wars, and by trying to outdo each other in displaying the greatness of their scholars, the grandeur of their buildings, and the beauty of their art.

Detail:

_____

Detail:

_____

Detail:

_____

Detail:

_____

Detail:

_____

Paraphrase:

_____

_____

_____

_____

_____

Part C - Review

Directions: Read the passage and then answer the questions.

During the 1400's, the Italians left the exploring of foreign lands to the Portuguese and the Spanish. Instead, they spent many years exploring a world of new ideas and attitudes. This period of exploration was called the Renaissance. During this time, Europeans moved from the Middle Ages into the modern world. The results were great and lasting accomplishments in science, literature, and the arts.

The Latin word "renaissance" means "rebirth." Using the ideas and art of ancient Greece and Rome, Italians began to focus on people. Human beings were put at the center of thought.

Important changes at the end of the Middle Ages contributed to the new focus. Instead of living on isolated manors, people began to live in towns where they could buy and sell food, cloth, spices, and much more. As a result, there was a large growth of merchants and shopkeepers. This middle class group no longer needed the rich nobles to support or protect them. They began to desire more education and to work toward their own goals. They made sure their children became educated in science, mathematics, philosophy, and the arts. Some devoted part of their wealth to the support of artists.

Of course, Italians benefited from this reform and even began to grow rich because of increased sea trade. Seaport cities became the crossroads of trading routes between Europe and the East. They also enjoyed the contacts they made with people from many different cultures who had a wide range of ideas.

A Renaissance man or woman is a person with many talents and accomplishments. The ideal "Renaissance man" used to be described as a true gentleman who is able to do many things well. He should be witty. He should be skilled in arms and such vigorous sports as hunting, swimming, and wrestling. He should be a scholar, a writer, an orator, a poet, and a musician. This ideal tells much about the spirit of the Renaissance. It was an age when people believed in their ability to achieve great things.

1. Which of the following titles BEST tells what this story is about?
    a. *Too Busy Changing to Explore*
    b. *What It Takes to Be a Renaissance Man*
    c. *Life in Italy During the Renaissance*
    d. *The Growing Middle Class of Italy*

2. Which of the following statements is a fact supported by information in the passage?
    a. Other countries followed the Italians' changing patterns of thought and behavior.
    b. In order to become rich in Italy, a man must be considered a Renaissance man.
    c. The country of Italy became weak because of their lack of exploration.
    d. The Renaissance period changed the lives of Italians.

3. The underlined word in the model sentence refers to:

Model: <u>They</u> also enjoyed the contacts they made with people from many different cultures with a wide range of ideas.

    a.   rich nobles

    b.   Italians

    c.   people in countries surrounding Italy

    d.   people traveling through the seaport cities of Italy

4. If the author were to add another line or two to the last paragraph, which of these choices would best belong?

    a.   Many men and women tried to reach the ideals of the Renaissance, but were not successful.

    b.   Leonardo da Vinci is often named as the perfect example of a Renaissance man. He was a painter, sculptor, writer, architect, inventor, engineer, and even something of a scientist.

    c.   A successful business man or woman of today would be considered the modern day Renaissance man.

    d.   If the grandfather in the family was considered to be a Renaissance man, then so was his son, his grandson, and his great-grandson.

5. What wouldn't you know if the second paragraph was left out?

    a.   that the seaport cities of Italy became very important

    b.   how the lives of the middle class changed during this period

    c.   the meaning of the Latin word "renaissance"

    d.   what subjects children studied in school

6. In writing this article, the author used:

    a.   unclear examples

    b.   specific details

    c.   questions and answers

    d.   famous quotes

7. The best possible meaning for the underlined word in the model sentence is:

Model: He should be skilled in <u>arms</u> and such vigorous sports as hunting, swimming, and wrestling.

    a.   part of a human limb between the shoulder and the wrist

    b.   weapons used in warfare

    c.   power of the law

    d.   part of a chair

Part D - Bonus

Pygmalion is a **mythological** character. He was a sculptor who didn't like women. He worked for a very long time to create a statue of a beautiful woman. After a while, he fell in love with the statue. The statue, of course, didn't love **Pygmalion**, which made him feel terrible. **Pygmalion** prayed to Venus, the goddess of love, to send him a woman just like his statue. Instead of sending **Pygmalion** a woman, Venus brought the statue to life. **Pygmalion** named the woman Galatea.

Lesson 57

Part A - Author's Purpose

Directions: Re-read the passage from Lesson 56 and then answer the questions.

Realistic art is just what the words suggest. It's realistic. If no one ever told you what a specific realistic painting was about, it would be easy to imagine the story behind the painting just by looking at it. A famous painting called *The Banjo Lesson* is an example of realistic art.

In this famous painting, a young boy is sitting on a man's knee, holding a banjo. Their heads are close together and they are both looking at the banjo. By looking at the expression on their faces, there is a feeling that the boy is getting encouragement from the man. Just by looking at the details of the picture it is quite clear that the boy and the man have a close relationship and they both share the experience of playing the banjo.

The artist who painted *The Banjo Lesson* is an African-American by the name of Henry O. Tanner. Although Tanner went to one of the finest art schools in the United States, he found it difficult to make a living by painting. Unfortunately, African-Americans were still not accepted as equals in the 1890s, even though slavery had ended decades earlier. Finally, Tanner decided to leave the United States and live and study in Paris. *The Banjo Lesson* was painted shortly after he arrived there.

Tanner and other realistic artists tried hard to make their paintings very true to life. Soon though, artists began to leave realism and look at new ways of representing the world on canvas.

Monet painted his "impressions" of what he saw instead of a detailed image. Vincent van Gogh wanted to show what his eyes saw, but also what his heart and his mind felt.

1. Why did the author include the second paragraph?

    _____

    _____

2. The author included the fourth paragraph so the reader would be informed about:

    _____

    _____

Part B- Paraphrase Paragraph

Directions: Read the paragraph below. Provide the information missing in the diagram. Then, write a paraphrase of the paragraph using your own words.

The Olympic Games are a form of competition we're familiar with today that has roots in ancient history. The tradition of lighting the Olympic flame, the oath of loyalty to the Olympic ideals, and the release of doves as a symbol of freedom began with an ancient Greek festival. Every four years athletes came from many city-states to compete in the Olympic Games. The winner of each competition was given a crown of olive leaves, but more importantly, he brought glory to his city. Women could not compete in the games. They were not even allowed to watch! However, women could technically compete in the chariot races since the horse's owner was considered the winner.

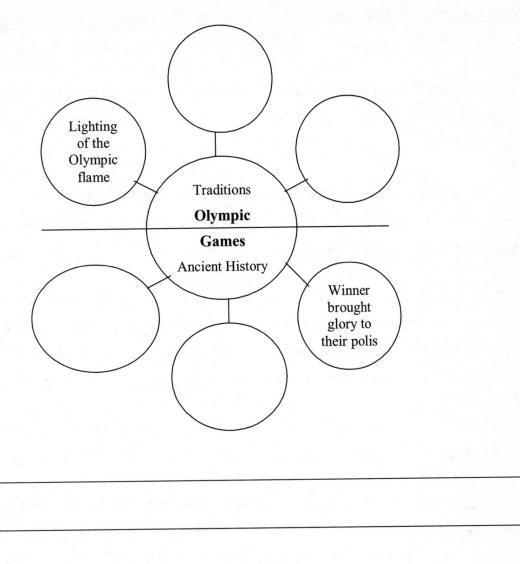

_____

_____

_____

_____

Part C - Review

Directions: Read the passage and then answer the questions.

Villagers in eastern China were planting trees when they made an amazing discovery. As they were digging up the earth with their shovels, they uncovered an ancient army of warriors. Not the kind of warrior that first comes to your mind, though. Each warrior was one foot tall and made of clay!

The clay soldiers were buried about 2,000 years ago, at a tomb site south of Beijing. Archaeologists are exploring the site, and so far they have found hundreds of the little soldiers. Along with the soldiers, they have found little horses, chariots, and other figures.

Archaeologists haven't found the actual tomb yet, so they don't know who was buried there. Most likely a member of a royal family is buried in the tomb. Only someone who was very important would have been buried along with a clay army.

As they continued to uncover the figures, they found that the figures were placed in the ground in marching order. At the front was the cavalry, with every soldier on horseback. Then came decorated chariots pulled by red horses. Behind the chariots marched the infantry. Alongside the soldiers were several figures representing musicians, including one with a drum.

As the figures are dug up, the archaeologists need to preserve them quickly. They are made of a type of fired clay called *terra cotta* and painted in bright colors that fade quickly in the air.

The burial site is spread over a large area. It may contain many pits like those that housed the clay soldiers. If so, many more figures may be found. These aren't the first figures to be found in China. In the 1970's researchers dug up more than 7,000 life-size soldiers at a royal tomb in central China. Another clay army was later found in the same region.

1. A good title for this passage would be:

    a. China's Hidden Treasures

    b. China's Underground Army

    c. The Big Dig

    d. Preservation of Terra Cotta

2. In the fourth paragraph the author used:

    a. questions and answers

    b. a diagram

    c. descriptions

    d. examples

3. Which one of the following words has about the same meaning as the underlined word?
   Model: Not the kind of warrior that first comes to your <u>mind</u>, though.

    a. opinion

    b. to pay attention

    c. to take charge

    d. the part of a person that feels, thinks, and reasons

4. The reader can tell from information in the passage that an archaeologist must:

    a. enjoy the outdoors

    b. be careful when handling items that have been dug up in order to preserve them

    c. be very interested hunting for buried for treasure

    d. have a great deal of knowledge about the layers of the earth

5. Choose the sentence that uses the underlined word in the same way as the model sentence.
   Model: As they continued to uncover the figures, they found that the figures were placed in the ground in marching <u>order</u>.

    a. When classifying plants or animals, <u>order</u> is below a class and above a family.

    b. Many times names are listed in alphabetical <u>order</u>.

    c. The general gave the <u>order</u> for the troops to leave the fort at sunrise.

    d. My <u>order</u> of fried eggs had to be sent back because I had asked for them to be scrambled.

6. This story mainly shows:

    a. the history of someone's life

    b. an accidental discovery

    c. how something was made

    d. places of interest to archeologist

7. How is the information in the first and last paragraph related?

    a. They compare and contrast the clay armies that were found in the 1970's and the armies that were found recently.

    b. They both describe two parts of China.

    c. They both explain the different ways clay armies have been discovered.

    d. They both give the exact year the different clay armies were discovered.

Part D - Bonus

If you come across the name **Pygmalion** while you are reading a fictional story, some character in the story probably changes dramatically, the same way **Pygmalion's** statue turned into a real woman.

BONUS REVIEW

Quatrain and **sestet** refer to the number of lines in a **stanza**. A **quatrain** has four lines and a **sestet** has six. **Quatrameter** refers to the number of **metrical feet** in a poem. A **trochee** is a type of **metrical foot**.

Lesson 58

Part A - Author's Purpose

Directions: Re-read the passage from Lesson 56 and then answer the questions.

Realistic art is just what the words suggest. It's realistic. If no one ever told you what a specific realistic painting was about, it would be easy to imagine the story behind the painting just by looking at it. A famous painting called *The Banjo Lesson* is an example of realistic art.

In this famous painting, a young boy is sitting on a man's knee, holding a banjo. Their heads are close together and they are both looking at the banjo. By looking at the expression on their faces, there is a feeling that the boy is getting encouragement from the man. Just by looking at the details of the picture it is quite clear that the boy and the man have a close relationship and they both share the experience of playing the banjo.

The artist who painted *The Banjo Lesson* is an African-American by the name of Henry O. Tanner. Although Tanner went to one of the finest art schools in the United States, he found it difficult to make a living by painting. Unfortunately, African-Americans were still not accepted as equals in the 1890s, even though slavery had ended decades earlier. Finally, Tanner decided to leave the United States and live and study in Paris. *The Banjo Lesson* was painted shortly after he arrived there.

Tanner and other realistic artists tried hard to make their paintings very true to life. Soon though, artists began to leave realism and look at new ways of representing the world on canvas. Monet painted his "impressions" of what he saw instead of a detailed image. Vincent van Gogh wanted to show what his eyes saw, but also what his heart and his mind felt.

1. Which of the following questions does the first paragraph answer?
    a. What famous painting is an example of realistic art?
    b. Why did Henry O. Tanner find it necessary to leave the United States in order to become successful?
    c. Who was *The Banjo Lesson* painted by?
    d. Which art school did Henry O. Tanner attend?

2. Paragraph three can be described as:
    a. an argument
    b. an instruction
    c. an explanation
    d. a conversation

Part B- Paraphrase Paragraph

Directions: Read the passage. Provide the information missing in the diagram. Then, write a paraphrase of the passage using your own words.

Drama during Greece's Classical period appeared in two forms--tragedy and comedy. Both forms originated in the city of Athens as part of a public festival

The subject matter of a tragedy was usually taken from epics and myths. In these plays, Greek heroes were the center of plots that revolved around the serious moments in their lives that were filled with conflict. They usually had a sad ending that often led to disaster and death. Tragedies were performed only in the morning at the festivals.

On the other hand, comedies were funny, usually had happy endings, and may have even made fun of famous people. Many comedies were less structured and the crowds felt free to talk and roam around the theater. Comedies were loud, happy events and were always full of jokes. Sometimes, the crowd would even yell at the actors on the stage!

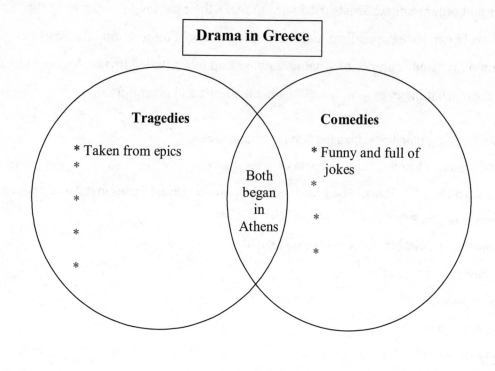

Drama in Greece

Tragedies

* Taken from epics
*

*

*

*

Both
began
in
Athens

Comedies

* Funny and full of
  jokes
*

*

*

_____

_____

_____

_____

Part C - Review

Directions: Read the passage and then answer the questions.

The Greek word "philosophy" means "love of wisdom." Socrates was a Greek philosopher and teacher who lived in Athens, Greece, in the 400s BC. Before Socrates, Greeks generally thought about the nature and origin of their world. Socrates taught that it was important for every person to question laws, social customs, and religious values. He urged Athenians to focus on how they should best live their lives.

Socrates spent much of his time in conversation with a wide range of Athenians, but mostly with young men. Socrates was not considered a professional teacher because he did not accept money from his listeners. As a result, he was very poor. Socrates was indifferent to physical comforts. He once stood in one spot for a day and night puzzling over a philosophical problem.

Many Athenians were annoyed by Socrates and his constant questioning of their beliefs. As a result of his criticism of the government, he was brought to trail and charged with trying to lead a revolt among the young people of Athens. He was convicted by a jury and sentenced to death. He could have escaped from prison, but he felt <u>obligated</u> to follow the court's decision, even if it was unjust. As the jailor brought the cup of hemlock, the poison which was used by the Athenians to carry out the death penalty, he remained calm.

Socrates wrote nothing, so the only knowledge we have of his ideas comes from other Greek writers. Plato, a student of Socrates, carried on his work by gathering together the ideas of Socrates and writing them down. Plato also founded the world's first university, known as the Academy. Greek ideas spread from Plato's Academy to Europe, Asia, and Africa. Today, students everywhere study the teachings of Plato and other Greek philosophers.

1. Which of the following would best summarize this passage?

    a. Socrates was unjustly punished for simply asking questions.

    b. The people of Athens shared common beliefs about religion, government, and customs. Socrates' questions about those beliefs not only made many of them unhappy, but also led to his death.

    c. Many of Socrates' questions are being discussed in countries around the world even today.

    d. Socrates was a teacher of philosophy in the world's first university.

2. Which of the following statements is a fact supported by information in the passage?

    a. Philosophy books contain some original handwritten notes that Socrates made during his time in prison.

    b. Afraid to let his ideas die, Socrates attempted to escape from prison many times.

    c. If it were not for the work of one of his students, Plato, many of Socrates' idea would not be studied today.

    d. Socrates is the most important philosopher of all time.

3. Which one of the following sentences uses the underlined word in the same way as the underlined word in the model sentence?

   Model: Socrates spent much of his time in conversations with a wide range of Athenians, but mostly with young men.

   a. The pioneers had a rough task ahead of them when crossing a mountain range.

   b. Our new electric range has a self-cleaning oven.

   c. There was quite a range of prices during the sale.

   d. Cattle were free to roam the range until fences were put up.

4. If the author were to add a question to the third paragraph, which of the following would best belong?

   a. Why didn't Socrates feel the need to escape?

   b. When did it become a crime to ask questions?

   c. Did everyone on the jury believe that Socrates was guilty?

   d. Did the young people of Athens ever plan a revolt against the government?

5. What does the author probably want you to remember the most from the third paragraph?

   a. Socrates remained calm even as he drank the hemlock.

   b. A jury found Socrates guilty.

   c. Socrates didn't try to escape from jail.

   d. The government was afraid of a revolt by the young people.

6. Which of the following definitions best fits the underlined word (obligated) in the third paragraph?

   a. afraid

   b. forced

   c. sense of duty

   d. act out of kindness

7. Which words from the story support the idea that it was **not** wrong of Socrates to question the beliefs of the Athenians?

   a. Many Athenians were annoyed by Socrates...

   b. The Greek word "philosophy" means "love of wisdom."

   c. Plato, a student of Socrates, carried on his work...

   d. ...even if it was unjust.

Part D - Bonus

George Bernard Shaw wrote a play in 1913 called "Pygmalion." The play was not about the **mythical** figure, **Pygmalion**. Rather, it was about a teacher in England who dramatically improves the speech of a poor and uneducated flower seller. You can probably guess why Shaw chose "Pygmalion" as the title of his play.

BONUS REVIEW

Here is an **idiom**: "A stitch in time saves nine." If a seam in a piece of your clothing starts to pull apart, and you don't sew it up right away (with a stitch), then the seam will pull apart further, and you'll have a bigger job. Maybe one stitch is all you need in the beginning, but you might end up needing nine stitches (or, a lot more than one) if you wait.

People use this **idiom** to mean: if a problem starts, try to solve it right away. Otherwise, it might grow into a much bigger problem.

These words describe the number of **metrical feet** in a line of poetry.

quatrameter: four metrical feet

pentameter: five metrical feet

octameter: eight metrical feet

Lesson 59

Part A - Author's Purpose

Directions: Re-read the passage from Lesson 56 and then answer the questions.

Realistic art is just what the words suggest. It's realistic. If no one ever told you what a specific realistic painting was about, it would be easy to imagine the story behind the painting just by looking at it. A famous painting called *The Banjo Lesson* is an example of realistic art.

In this famous painting, a young boy is sitting on a man's knee, holding a banjo. Their heads are close together and they are both looking at the banjo. By looking at the expression on their faces, there is a feeling that the boy is getting encouragement from the man. Just by looking at the details of the picture it is quite clear that the boy and the man have a close relationship and they both share the experience of playing the banjo.

The artist who painted *The Banjo Lesson* is an African-American by the name of Henry O. Tanner. Although Tanner went to one of the finest art schools in the United States, he found it difficult to make a living by painting. Unfortunately, African-Americans were still not accepted as equals in the 1890s, even though slavery had ended decades earlier. Finally, Tanner decided to leave the United States and live and study in Paris. *The Banjo Lesson* was painted shortly after he arrived there.

Tanner and other realistic artists tried hard to make their paintings very true to life. Soon though, artists began to leave realism and look at new ways of representing the world on canvas. Monet painted his "impressions" of what he saw instead of a detailed image. Vincent van Gogh wanted to show what his eyes saw, but also what his heart and his mind felt.

1. With which statement would the author probably agree?

   a. Realistic artists usually paint scenes from their childhood.

   b. Realistic art forms are the most popular among art critics.

   c. Most paintings don't become famous until the artist has died.

   d. People looking at realistic art may be reminded of people, things, or events they've experienced in their own lives.

2. Which of the following sayings would best fit this passage?

   a. Beauty is in the eye of the beholder.

   b. All's well that ends well.

   c. There's more than one way to skin a cat.

   d. To see is to believe.

Part B- Paraphrase Paragraph

Directions: Read the passage. Provide the information missing in the diagram. Then, write a paraphrase of the passage using your own words.

At the age of 18, he was a military commander, and at the age of 20 he was crowned king of Greece and western Asia. Add Egypt to the list of countries under his rule by the age of 24. At the age of 28 he conquered the Persian Empire, and at the age of 32 he died a legend.

As a small boy, Alexander the Great was taught by a wise, famous philosopher from Athens by the name of Aristotle. He learned to love philosophy and the Greek ways. His greatest wish was to spread the Greek legacy. As a talented general, he never lost a battle as he marched his armies across the Middle East, building city-states, all named Alexandria. By blending the Greek culture with the cultures of the Middle East, he gained the people's support along the way. The most famous city named Alexandria was built in the Nile Delta. It attracted scholars, sailors, and merchants. The city also boasted the world's first museums and libraries.

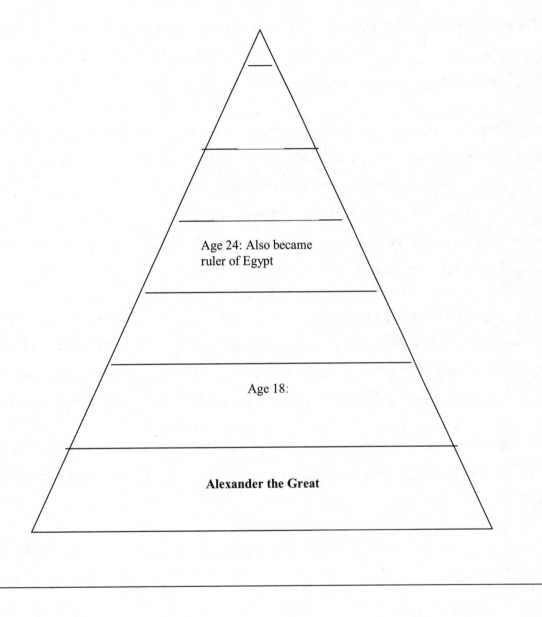

Age 24: Also became
ruler of Egypt

Age 18:

Alexander the Great

_____

_____

_____

_____

_____

Part C - Review

Directions: Read the passage and then answer the questions.

For ten years, the Greeks had attacked the city of Troy without success. The layout and structure of the city walls made the ancient city impossible to enter. The Greeks needed a war machine. They needed something new. So the Greeks <u>devised</u> a plan and put it to work.

The Greeks built a giant, wooden horse with a hollow belly. A handful of armed Greeks climbed into the hollow opening, and sealed it up. Meanwhile, the rest of the Greek army piled into their ships and sailed away. The Trojans came out of Troy to receive the huge horse they thought was an offering of peace. They placed wheels under the base of the horse and ropes were stretched about its neck to bring the gift inside the gates of Troy. The Trojans rejoiced at the thought of the Greek army running away as scared as rabbits!

The Trojans then decided to celebrate their victory long into the night. In the small hours of the morning, while everyone was asleep, the Greeks unsealed the belly of the horse, and climbed down from it. Silently, they killed the Trojan sentries at the city gates. The gates were then opened to the <u>bulk</u> of the Greek army. The Trojans had not seen the Greek fleet return to their shores.

Now, the Greeks were finally inside the city after ten years of useless battles. The Greeks finally had their chance at victory. By daylight, everyone in Troy was either dead, or held as a slave.

Today, the expression "a Trojan horse" is used to describe something that may seem good, but is really harmful.

1. This passage is mostly about:

    a.   the well-educated people of Troy who built a city that was impossible to enter

    b.   why the Greeks never gave up trying to enter the city of Troy

    c.   how the Greeks played a trick on the citizens of Troy

    d.   the days after the city of Troy was taken over by the Greek army

2. Which saying has the same or similar meaning as the expression "a Trojan horse"?

   a.   If at first you don't succeed try, try again.

   b.   a wolf in sheep's clothing

   c.   The bigger they are, the harder they fall.

   d.   He who laughs last laughs best.

3. Which one of the following definitions would best match the underlined word in the model sentence?
   Model: So the Greeks <u>devised</u> a plan and put it to work.

   a.   borrowed

   b.   designed

   c.   bought

   d.   altered

4. Using details from the passage, describe how the Trojan Horse was brought into the city of Troy.

   _____

   _____

   _____

5. Which one of the following definitions would best match the underlined word in the model sentence?
   Model: The gates were then opened to the <u>bulk</u> of the Greek army.

   a.   returning part

   b.   largest part

   c.   specialized part

   d.   smallest part

6. How many years had the Greeks attacked the city of Troy without success?

   a.   20

   b.   11

   c.   8

   d.   10

7. Which one of the following phrases does the author use to show that the Trojans were thinking the Greeks had been afraid of them?

    a. ...after ten years of useless battles.

    b. ...they thought was a peace offering.

    c. ...running away as scared as rabbits!

    d. ...piled into their ships and sailed away.

8. The passage doesn't exactly tell you the answer, but *the small hours of the morning* are probably:

    a. between the hours of 1:00 and 3:00 am

    b. between the hours of 9:00 and 11:00 am

    c. between the hours of 7:00 and 9:00 am

    d. between the hours of 11:00 pm and 1:00 am

9. Which character trait best describes the Trojans in dealing with the Trojan Horse?

    a. trusting

    b. boastful

    c. peaceful

    d. greedy

Part D - Bonus

In 1938, a movie called "Pygmalion" was released. The movie told the same story as the George Bernard Shaw play by the same name. Another famous **Pygmalion** story is "Pinocchio."

BONUS REVIEW

Words that end with similar—but not exactly the same—sounds are **partial rhymes**. Here are some examples of **partial rhymes**: lake and late, wish and wash.

Each of the following words could be a **trochaic foot** in a poem:

    e´lbow   dee´ply   se´quence   boo´klet   aw´kward

Each word has two syllables. The first syllable in each word is accented, and the second is unaccented. If you say words like this loudly, the accented syllable stands out clearly.

Lesson 61

Part A - Poetry

Here is the first stanza of a poem by Paul Lawrence Dunbar, entitled "Sympathy."

<u>Stanza 1</u>

I know what the caged bird feels, alas!

When the sun is bright on the upland slopes;

When the wind stirs soft through the springing grass,

And the river flows like a stream of glass;

When the first bird sings and the first bud opes,

And the faint perfume from its chalice steals-

I know what the caged bird feels!

As you know, in order to understand poems, you often have to read them more carefully than other types of writing. Here are some things you need to do to understand a poem:

1. Make sure you know what all the words mean.

    "Opes" is an out-of-date form of the word "opens."
    A "chalice" is a type of cup.
    One meaning of "steal" is "to move quietly or unobserved."

2. Look for **figurative language**: "...the river flows like a stream of glass" is an example of figurative language.

Part B - Poetry

Directions: Answer the questions about the first stanza of "Sympathy" in Part A.

1. The time of year identified in the first stanza is Spring. Which line in the stanza show that the most clearly?

_____

2. How might a bird in a cage feel when it hears other birds singing outside?

_____

3. Name one way that a river can be like a stream of glass.

_____

4. What does "its" refer to in the line "And the faint perfume from its chalice steals"?

_____

5. There are seven lines in the first stanza. The rhyming pattern of the first three lines is: a b a. What is the rhyming pattern for the remaining four lines?

_____

Part C - Review

Directions: Read the passage below and then answer the questions.

Do you know the saying "double-edged sword?" It's used to describe something that has two results, one good and one bad. Major scientific advances are often like that, offering humans wonderful benefits along with heavy responsibilities.

Take, for instance, the element radium. Radium is radioactive, meaning that it actively gives off particles smaller than atoms. These subatomic particles can be directed at unhealthy cells and used to cure cancer and tumors. But, exposure to radioactivity can also harm healthy cells and make you very sick. It can even kill you.

While reading about the element uranium and its release of radiation, Marie Curie got an idea. She began to test every known element for signs of radioactivity. She soon discovered that a mineral called *pitchblende* was more radioactive than pure uranium.

Marie and her husband began to separate radium from tons of pitchblende. Marie dissolved the powdered mineral and boiled it in huge metal pots for hours at a time. She and her husband used chemicals to separate the compounds, and then threw away everything that was not radioactive. It took four years to obtain a pure sample of radium.

During these years, the Curies breathed radioactive gas, ate radium in their food, and handled it with their bare hands. Scientists estimate that the radiation in their laboratory was one hundred times the amount considered safe today. Marie Curie's notebooks are still too radioactive to handle. The Curies observed in themselves the physical effects of radiation poisoning; extreme fatigue, burns that wouldn't heal, pains in their limbs, nagging colds, and coughs. But they also noticed that radiation harmed tumors more quickly than it harmed healthy cells. Radiation really was a double-edged sword. Too much was harmful, but careful use of radiation could actually cure some diseases. The world rejoiced at news of a productive <u>tool</u> for treating tumors. In 1903 the Curies received a <u>joint</u> Nobel Prize for their work.

After her husband's death in a carriage accident, Marie Curie continued their work alone. She also became the first female professor in France. During World War I, she helped equip ambulances with X-ray equipment that could be transported to the site of a battlefield. Thanks to her, some 1,100,000 wounded men received X-rays and were treated more effectively. She was the first woman awarded a Nobel Prize and the first person to win two Nobel Prizes, receiving one in physics and one in chemistry.

Marie Curie died on July 4, 1934, from leukemia that resulted from her long exposure to high energy radiation.

1. This passage is mostly about:
    a. the uses of uranium
    b. the Curies' work with radiation and the results of their work
    c. how Nobel Prizes are awarded
    d. the life of Marie Curie

2. Which sentence from the passage would support the model statement?
    Model: An item exposed to high levels of radiation will remain radioactive for a long period of time.

_____

_____

3. Choose the best possible meaning for the underlined word in the model sentence.

    Model: The world rejoiced at the news of a productive <u>tool</u> for treating tumors.

    a. machine

    b. method

    c. antibiotic

    d. research

4. Which of the following statements is an opinion?

    a. The dangers of using radioactive materials are much greater than the benefits.

    b. Marie Curie is responsible for helping save the lives of wounded men in World War I.

    c. Long exposure to radiation resulted in Marie Curie's death.

    d. Used in the correct way, radiation treatment is beneficial.

5. The article doesn't actually tell you, but Marie Curie probably learned about uranium and its release of radiation by reading:

    a. another scientist's diary

    b. a scientific article

    c. a letter from a good friend

    d. a chapter in a medical book about tumors

6. Which of the following situations may also be classified as "a double-edged sword"?

    a. eating too much fried food

    b. the invention of the telephone

    c. the discovery of penicillin

    d. the use of pesticides that can hurt people, but kill harmful insects

7. Which of the following is the correct order used by the Curies to separate radium from pitchblende?

    a. dissolve the powdered mineral; use chemicals to separate the compounds; throw out everything that is not radioactive; boil for hours

    b. dissolve the powdered mineral; boil for hours; use chemicals to separate the compounds; throw out everything that is not radioactive

    c. use chemicals to separate the compounds; boil for hours; dissolve the powdered mineral; throw out everything that is not radioactive

    d. dissolve the powdered mineral; use chemicals to separate the compounds; boil for hours; throw out everything that is not radioactive

8. The level of radiation in the Curies' laboratory was how many times higher than what is considered safe by today's standards?

    a.   one thousand

    b.   ten

    c.   one hundred

    d.   one million

9. Which of the following would make a good summary statement for this passage?

    a.   The Curies dedicated their lives to the good of mankind.

    b.   Successful scientists are honored by being awarded the Nobel Prize.

    c.   X-rays are the result of the work done by Marie Curie and her husband.

    d.   The higher the benefits of scientific discoveries, the more responsibilities come with it.

10. Which of the following phrases from the passage is used to define the word "subatomic"?

    a.   Major scientific advances...

    b.   ...exposure to radioactivity

    c.   ...particles smaller than atoms.

    d.   ...signs of radioactivity

11. Which sentence from the passage support the meaning of the saying "double-edged sword"?

_____

_____

Part D - Bonus

Hyperbole is an exaggeration made on purpose. **Hyperbole** is pronounced like this:

   hi PER bow lee

You have probably used **hyperbole** yourself many times. Here is a common example of **hyperbole**: "If I've told you once, I've told you a million times: stop doing that!"

Hyperbole comes from Greek. When a person is "hyper," that person has an excess of energy. **Hyper** means "excess."

BONUS REVIEW

Pygmalion is a mythological character, a sculptor who worked for a very long time to create a statue of a beautiful woman. Venus, the goddess of love, brought the statue to life.

Lesson 62

Part A- Poetry

Here is the second stanza of "Sympathy," by Paul Lawrence Dunbar.

<u>Stanza 2</u>

I know why the caged bird beats his wing

Till its blood is red on the cruel bars;

For he must fly back to his perch and cling

When he fain would be on the bough a-swing;

And a pain still throbs in the old, old scars

And they pulse again with a keener sting-

I know why he beats his wing!

"Fain" is an out-of-date word that means "preferably" or "rather."
"A-swing" is an out-of-date way of saying "swinging."
One meaning of "keen" is "intense."

Part B - Poetry

Directions: Answer the questions about the second stanza of "Sympathy" in Part A.

1. The mood in the second stanza is dark or unpleasant. What are some of the words that create this mood?

\
\

2. Why is the bird in the cage beating its wings until they're bloody?

\
\

3. The bird has to sit on its perch in the cage, but where would it rather be sitting?

\
\

4. How did the bird probably get its old scars?

_____

5. What is the rhyming pattern for the second stanza?

_____

Part C - Review

Directions: Read the passage below and then answer the questions.

Australia, which is a country, is also the second driest continent. Only Antarctica gets less precipitation than Australia. <u>It</u> is home to the Gibson, the Great Sandy, the Great Victoria, and the Simpson deserts. Together they cover about one-third of the country.

The middle section of Australia is an area of great curiosity. This area, covering a little more than 75 percent of the country, is known as the Outback. The word outback comes from the phrase "out in the back country." The land and climate in most of the Outback is harsh and unsettled, with little rainfall. Millions of years of weathering and erosion in the Outback have resulted in a flattened landscape and poor soil. In the Outback, you'll find large deserts with plant-covered sand dunes. There are also large areas of dry grassland that have been used for grazing sheep and cattle.

Less than ten percent of all the people living in Australia make their homes in the Outback. Those who do live there live many miles from each other. They must be hardy and self-reliant enough to deal with the isolation. Radio and television, which is available by satellite, help reduce the feeling of loneliness. Telephones allow people to keep in touch with neighbors who are too far away to visit easily.

Life for children in the Outback may be quite different than the life you are used to. For example, you probably walk to school, ride the bus, or you might be driven to school by your parents. Most children living in the Outback live far away from any school. They are taught at home from a program called *School of the Air*. Assignments are given out over the radio, and then the children mail in their homework to be graded. The radio is also used to call for help when people are sick. *The Royal Flying Doctor Service* (RFDS) provides doctors, nurses, and dentists to care for the people living in the Outback. Some of the doctors fly long distances every year caring for patients who are scattered far apart.

1. Which of the following sentences expresses the author's specific purpose?

    a. The author's purpose is to inform the reader about the way of life in the part of Australia known as the Outback.

    b. The author's purpose is to inform the reader about the importance of airplanes in Australia.

    c. The author's purpose is to persuade the reader that people living in the Outback like to be left alone.

    d. The author's purpose is to explain to the reader the different ways children in the world receive an education.

2. What information would you **not** find in this passage?

    a. the fact that Australia is a continent as well as a country

    b. which animals, if any, are native to the Outback

    c. the landscape of the Outback

    d. how medical services are delivered to the people living in the Outback

3. The best human character trait that could be used to describe the Outback would probably be:

    a. friendly

    b. unforgiving

    c. scary

    d. generous

4. Choose the word that means the same or close to the same as the underlined word in the model sentence.
    Model: They must be hardy and self-reliant enough to deal with the isolation.

    a. remoteness

    b. dry conditions

    c. quiet

    d. economy

5. In paragraph four, how did the author involve the reader in the paragraph?

    a. By asking questions that the reader could answer by reading an article about different types of education.

    b. By asking questions and providing the answers.

    c. By using the word "you" in examples of how the reader might arrive at school.

    d. By explaining in detail a scene that the reader could easily picture in her mind.

6. This passage would most likely be found in a book titled:

    a.   Famous Deserts of the World

    b.   Life in the Australian Outback

    c.   Living Alone

    d.   Teaching in the Outback of Australia

7. There's enough information in this passage to show that:

    a.   Australia is a wonderful vacation spot.

    b.   Few people can handle the demands and adjustments that need to be made in order to live in the Outback.

    c.   People living in the Outback are ignored by other Australians.

    d.   You can only live in the Outback if you were born there.

8. In the first paragraph, the underlined word "it" refers to:

    a.   the climate

    b.   the Simpson Desert

    c.   Antarctica

    d.   Australia

9. In which of the following sentences is the underlined word used in the same way as the underlined word in the model sentence?

    Model: Together they cover about one-third of the country.

    a.   We always cover our firewood with plastic so it doesn't get wet.

    b.   Our family took cover in the basement during the tornado warning.

    c.   My best friend is going to cover our neighborhood, and I'll look in the surrounding blocks for his dog.

    d.   The insurance will cover the damage done to our car after the accident.

10. In the passage, the words "harsh" and "unsettled" are used to describe to the reader the Australian:

    a.   land

    b.   people

    c.   climate

    d.   way of life

11. The word "self-reliant" refers to people who are probably:

    a.   afraid of living alone

    b.   good at solving their own problems

    c.   interested in studying nature

    d.   anthropologists studying the different ways people in the world live

Part D - Bonus Review

A **myth** is a story with heroic characters and deities, such as **Pygmalion**. To understand what you are reading, you sometimes have to know about some **mythological** characters.

Lesson 63

Part A - Poetry

Here is the third stanza of "Sympathy," by Paul Lawrence Dunbar.

<u>Stanza 3</u>

I know why the caged bird sings, ah me,

When his wing is bruised and his bosom sore,-

When he beats his bars and he would be free;

It is not a carol of joy or glee,

But a prayer that he sends from his heart's deep core,

But a plea, that upward to Heaven he flings-

I know why the caged bird sings!

The bird's "bosom" is its chest.

A "carol" is a song, like a Christmas carol, and is usually a happy song.

To "plea" means to ask for something very sincerely.

The author, Paul Lawrence Dunbar, was an American born in 1872. He died at the age of thirty-three. He was the first African-American to be recognized internationally as a great poet and novelist. Slavery was over in America when Dunbar was born, but most African-Americans were still living with poverty and prejudice.

Part B - Poetry

Directions: Answer the questions about the third stanza of "Sympathy" in Part A.

1. What is the rhyming pattern of the third stanza?

2. Why does the bird in the cage sing?

_____

3. This whole poem is a **metaphor**. A bird in a cage is being compared to something. What could the poet be comparing the bird with?

_____

Part C - Review

Directions: Read the passage below and then answer the questions.

The Latin word "jury" is defined as a group of people chosen by law, sworn to consider the facts of a case and decide what is the truth. During a legal trial, the jury will listen to both sides tell their stories and then decide if the person on trial is guilty or not guilty. In the United States, the law states that an accused person is considered innocent until proven guilty in a court of law.

Before jury trials existed, two main ways of deciding guilt or innocence were *trial by battle* or *the ordeal*. During a trial by battle, the accused person battled the person accusing him of the crime. Winning the battle proved innocence, while losing showed guilt. One example of an ordeal required the accused person to swallow a large piece of meat. The person was innocent if he was successful and guilty if he was unsuccessful.

During the Athenian Age of Pericles, all male citizens were invited to serve on juries. Pericles arranged for jury members to be paid. Because of this, the poor could serve as part of a jury as easily as could the rich. Although this was a good beginning to the democratic form of government, it was a long way from modern democracies. Democracy in Athens did not give freedom to everyone. Only male citizens were allowed to vote or take part in the Assembly. Although women were citizens, they were not allowed to vote. The other half of Athens' population, slaves, were not allowed to have any part in the government either.

The legend of Athenian democracy had a great influence on the birth of the American, as well as many other modern, democratic forms of government.

1. Put an **X** next to the three statements that just tell details from the passage. Then, write **MI** next to the statement that is a good main idea statement. Finally, write **TG** next to the statement that is TOO GENERAL to be a good main idea statement for this passage.

    a. _____ In a court of law, a jury decides if a person is guilty or not guilty after hearing the evidence.

    b. _____ Even though in early democratic governments justice was not always fair, and equal rights didn't apply to everyone, the foundation for modern forms of democratic government was laid.

    c. _____ It was important to Pericles that all males had a voice in the government, so jury members were paid.

    d. _____ Juries play an important role in a democracy

    e. _____ Before the jury system, the process of deciding guilt or innocence was often cruel and unjust.

2. The author's main purpose is to:

    a. persuade the reader of the importance of serving on a jury

    b. explain the justice system in the United States

    c. describe early forms of justice

    d. explain the influence of Pericles and the Athenians on today's system of justice and democracy

3. In paragraph one, the word "states" means:

    a. to express in words

    b. an area of land inside a country

    c. to argue

    d. to pretend

4. With which statement would the author probably agree?

    a. The jury system of today can be greatly improved.

    b. Although it may not be perfect, trial by jury is a great improvement over the ordeal and the trial by battle forms of justice.

    c. The Age of Pericles had little influence on modern democracy.

    d. Many times, an accused person will not tell the truth during the trial.

5. The author of the passage helps the reader learn about justice by:

    a. explaining how a jury is chosen

    b. comparing a past form of determining guilt or innocence to the present system

    c. showing the development and changes in the justice system on a timeline

    d. giving details of the democratic system during the Age of Pericles

6. Which group of words best applies to this passage?

   a. clever, cruel, adventurous

   b. fear, anger, guilt

   c. strength, justice, innocence

   d. truth, justice, democracy

7. Which of the following groups were not allowed to vote during the Pericles form of Ancient Greek democracy?

   a. poor males and women

   b. men and women under the age of 30

   c. slaves and women

   d. slaves and poor males

8. Why was it important for Pericles to pay the members of the jury?

   a. members of the jury would be more fair when making their decision

   b. the opinions of the poor as well as the rich could be represented on a jury

   c. serving on a jury would take them away from their regular paying jobs so no one would want to be on a jury

   d. jury pay was taxed more heavily than their regular income so it meant more money for the government

9. Which information about a jury is **not** mentioned in the first paragraph? (**Note**: there are TWO correct answers.)

   a. how old a person must be in order to be on a jury

   b. definition of the word jury

   c. number of people on a jury

   d. responsibilities of people sitting on a jury

10. What information from the first paragraph is probably the most important?

_____

_____

Part D - Bonus Review

A **stanza** of a poem with four lines is called a **quatrain**.

A **stanza** of a poem with six lines is called a **sestet**.

An **internal rhyme** is a word within a line that rhymes with another word at the end of the line.

The following line has an **internal rhyme**:

It doesn't matter, the former or the latter.

Lesson 64

Part A - Poetry

Directions: Read "Sympathy" once again. You are going to have a discussion on this poem. There are two discussion questions:

1. This poem is about how it feels to not have freedom. Which people in the world right now do not have freedom?

2. People can be "enslaved" to many things. A drug addict, for example, is a slave to drugs. A person who watches television a great deal can be thought of as a slave to television. What types of things might students in school be enslaved to?

Stanza 1

I know what the caged bird feels, alas!

When the sun is bright on the upland slopes;

When the wind stirs soft through the springing grass,

And the river flows like a stream of glass;

When the first bird sings and the first bud opes,

And the faint perfume from its chalice steals-

I know what the caged bird feels!

Stanza 2

I know why the caged bird beats his wing

Till its blood is red on the cruel bars;

For he must fly back to his perch and cling

When he fain would be on the bough a-swing;

And a pain still throbs in the old, old scars

And they pulse again with a keener sting-

I know why he beats his wing!

<u>Stanza 3</u>

I know why the caged bird sings, ah me,

When his wing is bruised and his bosom sore,-

When he beats his bars and he would be free;

It is not a carol of joy or glee,

But a prayer that he sends from his heart's deep core,

But a plea, that upward to Heaven he flings-

I know why the caged bird sings!

Discussion questions.

1. This poem is about how it feels to not have freedom. Which people in the world right now do not have freedom?

2. People can be "enslaved" to many things. A drug addict, for example, is a slave to drugs. A person who watches television a great deal can be thought of as a slave to television. What types of things might students in school be enslaved to?

Part B - Review

Directions: Read the passage below and then answer the questions.

Perhaps one of the most <u>extravagant</u> rulers of France was King Louis XIV. He liked to refer to himself as "the Sun King." He actually believed that just like the planets revolved around the sun, the world circled around him. During his reign, France became one united nation-state instead of a collection of provinces ruled by various barons.

Just outside of the city of Paris, Louis had an enormous palace built full of dazzling mirrors, chandeliers, and works of art. Plays and concerts were held constantly at the palace. Meanwhile, outside the palace, France was becoming not only the most powerful, but the most elegant and most advanced country in Europe. Other countries were demanding their fine linens, porcelain, and decorations. The upper classes throughout the world began to speak the French language. French literature, music, and some of their customs were highly thought of in Europe as well as America.

The beautiful Marie Antoinette was the willful queen of France. At the age of 15 she married Louis, the dauphin, or crown prince, of France. When his grandfather died in 1774, the prince became king Louis XVI and Marie Antoinette became the queen.

The Queen liked to spend money, and she ended up wastefully spending fortunes. When she and some of her "fine friends" became bored, they liked to dress in expensive costumes and pretend that they were common milkmaids and shepherds. During that same period of time, unemployment and hunger were widespread among the lower classes. Because of her style, they thought of the Queen as spoiled, and they blamed her for their miseries. Although it may not be true, they could easily believe the legend that when the Queen was told that the people had no bread, she quipped, "Then let them eat cake."

Within a few decades, the lives of the King and Queen would change dramatically as the Enlightenment ideals of natural rights and relations between the people and their rulers spread. The final straw came when Louis XVI decided to tax the two upper social classes because of financial problems. An Assembly meeting was called by the clergy and the nobility to reject the taxes, and as a way to show their power. But, the third class, which was by far the largest, had begun to hear about a new country where there were no kings or nobles. When they realized they weren't being listened to in the Assembly, they took matters into their own hands. The large lower class began making speeches and declared themselves the National Assembly. They took an oath to fight for equal rights for every citizen, as well as freedom of religion and the right to a fair trail for everyone. King Louis XVI reacted in two ways. He ordered the two upper classes to join the Assembly, but he also sent thousands of troops to frighten the Assembly. The plan didn't work. Instead of becoming frightened, people became angry. They roamed the streets gathering weapons and a riot soon broke out. The French Revolution had begun.

A few months later, still hungry and angry, thousands of revolutionaries and workers from the Paris marketplace broke into the palace and captured the King, the Queen, and their young son. The royals tried to escape, but were soon captured and taunted by angry mobs. While they were in prison, fighting continued among those in power. Thousands died during the revolution, including the King and Queen. The King was beheaded in the main square in Paris among cheering crowds. Marie Antoinette was charged with treason, brought before a revolutionary court, and treated like a commoner. Throughout her trial the Queen remained serene and dignified. She calmly heard her sentence pronounced. As her husband had, she went to her death on the guillotine.

1. Place the letters **MI** next to the statement that would be a good main idea statement. Place the letter **X** next to the three statements that are supporting details.

   a. _____ The King and Queen spent large amounts of money on their palace and their excessive lifestyle.

   b. _____ The lower class took an oath to fight for equal rights for every citizen, as well as freedom of religion and the right to a fair trail for everyone.

   c. _____ King Louis XVI and Queen Marie Antoinette lived a lifestyle that angered the majority of the French people enough that they were overthrown and eventually put to death.

   d. _____ A legend says that Marie Antoinette said, "Then let them eat cake."

2. Which of the following statements is a **fact** supported by the passage?

   a. If given a second opportunity, the King and Queen would probably change the way they lived their lives.

   b. Queen Marie Antoinette showed calm and proud characteristics.

   c. King Louis XVI and Queen Marie Antoinette were blamed unfairly for the troubles experienced by the third class of people.

   d. When the troops arrived at the Assembly meeting, the people were frightened enough to stop protesting.

3. The passage doesn't actually tell you the answer, but the third class of people mentioned in the fifth paragraph were probably:

   a. women

   b. slaves

   c. working people

   d. barons

4. Which of the following statements would make a good main idea statement for the second paragraph?

   a. Many rich and famous people visited France during the reign of Louis XIV.

   b. The upper class of society began to speak French.

   c. Many countries wanted French fine linens and decorations.

   d. During the reign of Louis XIV, France became a powerful influence across Europe and America.

5. As used in the first paragraph, which of the following pairs of words have similar meanings?

    a. around and circled

    b. revolved and circled

    c. united and various

    d. king and baron

6. In the sixth paragraph the phrase "...had begun to hear about a new country where their were no kings or nobles" probably refers to:

    a. Germany

    b. America

    c. Mexico

    d. Canada

7. Choose the best meaning for the underlined word in the model sentence.

    Model: Although it may not be true, they could easily believe the legend that when the Queen was told that the people had no bread, she quipped, "Then let them eat cake."

    a. quick and rude comment

    b. loudly spoken order

    c. softly spoken reply

    d. well mannered remark

8. This passage could be an example of a:

    a. biography

    b. myth

    c. letter

    d. history report

Lesson 66

Part A - Review

Directions: Read the passage below and then answer the questions.

Near the surface of the water, in the middle depths, and on the ocean floor live several hundred thousand kinds of plants and animals. The size of the ocean, the temperature, the currents, and the water pressure, along with the depth of the water, determine where different kinds of sea life are found. Other important factors are the amount of light, the amount of nutrients, and the characteristics of the sea floor.

One of largest groups of organisms living in the ocean is plankton. The word plankton comes from the Greek work *planktos*, which means "to wander." This describes the life of plankton quite well. They are a groups of plants and animals that have little or no ability to swim. Instead, they float and are carried by the currents and tides of the water. Most of them are tiny enough that they cannot be seen. But one kind of plankton, the jellyfish, is quite large. The plankton family has a varied lifestyle. Some of them spend only a part of their lives as plankton. They may begin their lives as eggs and develop into swimming adults. Other examples of sea life that spend part of their lives as plankton are crabs, snails, and clams that later live on the sea floor. Plant members of the plankton family are very small. They use the energy from sunlight to make food. In turn, they become the food for many forms of life that live in the ocean.

Larger animals that can swim usually have backbones. Sharks, reptiles such as turtles, and many types of fish live in the open waters. Other marine mammals, such as whales, dolphins, porpoises, and seals, are popular members of this group. Disagreement exists over whether or not people should be able to hunt seals and whales. The whale population has been drastically reduced in recent years. Because of this, laws have been passed to stop the killing of whales and other marine animals.

There are also certain plants and animals that live on the ocean floor. They depend on the sea floor for shelter. Eels and shrimp are examples of animals that feed on other organisms on the sea floor and burrow into soft mud along the bottom. Plants, such as kelp or brown algae, also live on the sea floor. Sponges and colorful corals can be found on the floor of oceans in tropical areas.

Deep sea life is quite mysterious. These organisms have made adaptations that allow them to <u>survive</u> the permanently cold and dark water where there is very little food. Fish living on the bottom of the deep sea have very small eyes, or no eyes at all. A mystery to biologists is certain deep-sea squids that have one eye larger than the other. Because of the lack of food on the ocean floor, many fish that live there are quite small. Others have very long teeth to snag their prey, while others have a light-producing organ that attracts prey.

1. Write a sentence that summarizes what this passage is mostly about.

_____

_____

_____

2. In this passage, the word <u>survive</u> means:

   a. grow larger

   b. remain alive

   c. ignore

   d. adapt

3. Which of the following is a **fact** supported by information in this passage?

   a. There are non-swimming animals in the ocean.

   b. Whales are the most popular type of sea mammal.

   c. Sea life that live in the deepest part of the ocean have huge eyes to let in more light.

   d. There are as many different kinds of life in the sea as there are varieties of life in the rainforest.

4. The purpose of this passage is to:

   a. persuade people that killing whales and other sea mammals should stop

   b. tell a story about diving for coral on the ocean floor

   c. describe the lifestyles of the plant and animal life in different depths of the ocean

   d. explain how sea life moves through the water

5. Which type of sea life has one eye larger than the other?

   a. squid

   b. tuna

   c. whales

   d. jellyfish

6. The word "plankton" comes from which language?

    a. Latin

    b. Greek

    c. Spanish

    d. French

7. The passage doesn't tell you the answer, but using information from the fifth paragraph you can tell that biologists study:

    a. human behavior

    b. weather

    c. energy forms

    d. animal life

8. Sponges and corals make their home:

    a. on the rocks near shore

    b. on the sea floor of all oceans

    c. on the sea floor of tropical oceans

    d. floating on the surface of the water

9. Which of the following belongs to the plankton family?

    a. eels

    b. jellyfish

    c. sea lions

    d. shrimp

10. Which of the following does **not** determine where a variety of sea life will make its home?

    a. water temperature

    b. human activity in the water

    c. food supply

    d. amount of light

11. Which details from the passage support the model sentence?

    Model: The plankton family differs greatly from the other forms of life found in the ocean.

    _____

    _____

    _____

Part B - Bonus Review

This is a **cognitive map**. It shows the organization of ideas.

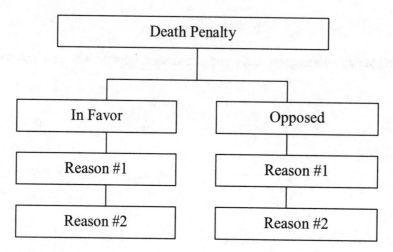

Quatrain and **sestet** refer to the number of lines in a **stanza**. A **quatrain** has four lines and a **sestet** has six.

Quatrameter refers to the number of **metrical feet** in a poem. A **trochee** is a type of **metrical foot**.

Lesson 67 Review

Part A - Review

Directions: Read the passage below and then answer the questions.

As the only animals with feathers and wings, their ability to fly has fascinated people for centuries. Their colors, sweet songs, and sense of freedom have been the inspiration for song writers, poets, and painters. They have also been used as a symbols of wisdom, peace, and strength. Read on and find out about some unusual birds that are fascinating in an many ways.

The hoatzin is known as the stink bird, and for good reason. This chicken-size bird has extremely bad breath! The hoatzin lives in the tropical forests of South America, and it has an unusual diet. While most birds eat insects, seeds, and berries, the hoatzin eats leaves, shoots, and buds. These plant materials have fibers and chemicals that most birds can't digest. The hoatzin has a special chamber in its digestive tract, like a cow, where bacteria break down the tough plant materials. Unfortunately, the bacteria also produce a lot of smelly gasses which the hoatzin burps up.

Oil birds are related to whippoorwills, goatsuckers, and nightjars, but look more like an owl. They spend most of their time roosting or flying, because their feet are poorly developed for walking. Like a bat, the oilbird spends daylight hours deep in dark caves. They get around with the help of echolocation, which is a kind of natural sonar system. Oil birds, which live in the northern parts of South America and the island of Trinidad, make clicking noises as they fly. The clicks bounce off the walls of the cave and the echoes allow the bird to judge where the walls are. At night, oil birds leave their caves and feast on fruit. Adults can grow to be more than a foot long, with wingspans up to 3 feet. Until their feathers grow in, baby birds are grossly fat, weighing up to twice as much as adults. The fat of these birds was once boiled down to make oil for torches.

Hawks, snakes, and other predators don't bother the hooded pitohui. This songbird, which lives on the Pacific Ocean island of New Guinea, has poisonous plumage. It has an orange-brown body with black wings, head, and tail. Oddly enough, its color pattern resembles the monarch butterfly, which is also poisonous. Its skin and feathers are laced with toxic chemicals that taste terrible, so predators leave it alone. Many insects, frogs, fish, and reptiles secrete poisons to keep enemies away. But the hooded pitohui is the only bird known to have this defense. Like many other poisonous animals, the pitohui has bold coloring. In the animal world, it is often a warning to predators to keep away.

Spoonbills are related to herons, storks, and flamingos. The spoonbill came by it's name naturally. Its bill is shaped like a long-handled serving spoon. The spoonbill is a wading bird that feeds in shallow waters. The bird partially opens its beak and sweeps it from side to side through the water, searching for small fish, water insects, and small crabs. Because the bill is sensitive, the bird knows when it has picked up something good to eat. The spoonbill also uses its bill to make loud clapping noises when it returns to its nest and greets its mate. Spoonbills live in warm, marshy areas around the world.

1. Write a summary paragraph of the above passage.

_____

_____

_____

_____

2. Compare the monarch butterfly and the hooded pitohui.

_____

_____

3. Choose the best meaning for the underlined word in the model sentence.

   Model: Its skin and feathers are laced with <u>toxic</u> chemicals that taste terrible, so predators leave it alone.

   a. strong smelling

   b. poisonous

   c. organic

   d. invisible

4. The main purpose of this passage is to:

   a. inform the reader about unusual birds

   b. explain to the reader the defenses used by many birds against their enemies

   c. explain to the reader how beauty can sometimes be used as a warning

   d. persuade the reader that bird watching can be enjoyable

5. Which sentence in paragraph four would probably lead you to believe that spoonbills have long legs?

   a. The spoonbill is a wading bird that feeds in shallow waters.

   b. Spoonbills live in warm, marshy areas around the world.

   c. Spoonbills are related to herons, storks, and flamingos.

   d. Its bill is shaped like a long-handled serving spoon.

6. At first sight the hooded pitohui probably:

    a.   looks very bright and attractive

    b.   is hard to see because it blends into its surroundings

    c.   warns its attackers to stay away

    d.   runs away to find shelter

7. How did the oilbird get its name?

    a.   It is one of the few birds that can survive the effects of an oil spill.

    b.   Their fat was once boiled to produce oil for torches.

    c.   Their feathers produce enough oil to make their bodies too slippery for enemies to hang on to.

    d.   Their feathers are highly prized for their oil content, which is used to make many expensive lotions.

8. Echolocation involves which one of the five senses?

    a.   hearing

    b.   taste

    c.   sight

    d.   smell

9. Which of the following titles BEST tells what this story is about?

    a.   Beauty May Be Only Skin Deep

    b.   Birds of an Unusual Feather Flock Together

    c.   Songbirds

    d.   Native Birds of South America

10. Which of the following is a **fact** expressed in this passage?

    a.   Birds with unusual names can be found in all warm climates.

    b.   The cow and the hoatzin have similar digestive systems.

    c.   Most songbirds are not bothered by hawks and eagles.

    d.   Spoonbills are related to herons, storks, and bats.

Part B - Bonus Review

Here is a **stanza** from a Paul Lawrence Dunbar poem:

> He was a poet who wrote clever verses,
>
> And folks said he had fine poetical taste;
>
> But his father, a practical farmer, accused him
>
> Of letting the strength of his arm go to waste.

This **stanza** is a **quatrain**. The **rhyming pattern** is: a b c b.

Lesson 68 Review

Part A - Review

Directions: Read the passage below and then answer the questions.

Stars are made of the same chemical elements that make up humans and other objects on Earth. The elements in the stars, however, exist in a different physical state than those found on Earth. The chemical atoms from elements found on Earth combine to form water, carbon dioxide, and other molecules that make up the human body. On stars, temperatures are so hot that molecules like the ones in our body cannot exist. Instead, the atoms in stars exist as a hot gas called *plasma*. The two most common elements in the universe can be found in a star. About 90 percent of the atoms in a star are hydrogen and 9 percent are helium.

When stars grow old, they explode and scatter different elements throughout space. These elements become the building blocks of new stars and planets. The Hubble Space Telescope (HST) has looked deep into the heart of our galaxy to the Milky Way. The Milky Way is where new stars are born when huge clouds of gas collide. Normally, we can't see these star <u>plants</u> because space dust and light from other stars block our view. But the HST has an infrared camera that can peer right through the dust and light to observe two massive clusters of young stars. In a few million years, gravity will pull these clusters apart. But right now, they are the brightest star clusters in our galaxy. Scientists hope that they will help unlock the secrets of how stars form.

Stars are packed like sardines in the Arches Cluster. This cluster is about 2 million years old, which is very young for an item in space. It includes 150 of the brightest stars known in the Milky Way. At least a dozen of the stars are 100 times more massive than our sun. The Quintuplet Cluster is about 4 million years old. Its stars are more scattered than those in the Arches Cluster. Many of these stars are on the verge of exploding into supernovas. They include the Pistol Star, which is the brightest known star in the Milky Way.

The nearest large galaxy to the Milky Way galaxy is about 2.2 million light-years away. The Andromeda galaxy is about one and a half times larger than the Milky Way galaxy. But more than a dozen small galaxies are closer. Two of the closest small galaxies are ten times closer than the Andromeda galaxy, and they are ten times smaller. Astronomers think that these small galaxies orbit our own galaxy much like the moon orbits Earth.

There are also about a dozen very faint, very small galaxies. Examples are "Leo" and "Sagittarius," which are named after the constellations in which they are seen. One of these dwarf galaxies is so close that it is invading our own galaxy. The dwarf galaxy orbits around the center of the Milky Way and may be leftover from the Milky Way's birth.

1. Which sentence **best** summarizes the story?

    a. The Hubble Space Telescope has made the research of space possible.

    b. The Milky Way may one day combine with smaller galaxies to become the largest galaxy containing planets.

    c. Although scientists have unraveled many of the mysteries about stars, there is still much information yet to be discovered.

    d. All matter in the universe is made of elements found on earth.

2. Stars can best be described as:

    a. individuals that make up galaxies

    b. points of light that appear to twinkle at night

    c. an extremely hot mixture of hydrogen and helium atoms that exist in the form of a gas

    d. clouds of dust and light

3. There is enough information in this passage to show that:

   a. Scientists know how stars are formed.

   b. An astronomer is a scientist who studies stars and galaxies.

   c. Dwarf galaxies all contain constellations.

   d. Orbiting around something is the only movement found in space.

4. In the passage, the quotation marks around "Leo" and "Sagittarius" refer to:

   a. names of constellations and galaxies

   b. the scientists that record information seen through the Hubble Space Telescope

   c. names of telescopes and space stations

   d. names of planets and galaxies

5. You would most likely find this passage in a/an:

   a. book about Roman gods

   b. scientist's journal

   c. book of little know facts and trivia

   d. encyclopedia

6. Which of the following statements is a **fact** supported by information in the passage?

   a. The same form of elements exist in a star and in the human body.

   b. The sun is the biggest star.

   c. Scientists have been able to observe other galaxies by using the Hubble Space Telescope.

   d. The amount of years we use to label something ancient here on earth would be used to label something young in space.

7. Which of the following phrases is part of the sentence in the passage that tells the reader which galaxy contains the planet Earth?

   a. ......orbit our own galaxy...

   b. Its stars are more scattered...

   c. ......invading our own galaxy.

   d. ...deep into the heart of our galaxy,...

8. Which of these questions does the third paragraph answer?

   a. What do exploding stars become?

   b. What is the closest galaxy to the Milky Way?

   c. Why is it difficult for scientists to see the birth of stars?

   d. Which element makes up 90 percent of the atoms in a star?

9. Choose the sentence that uses the underlined word in the same way as the model sentence.

    Model: Normally, we can't see these star <u>plants</u> because space dust and light from other stars block our view.

    a. The <u>plants</u> go on sale at the end of this month.

    b. His aim is much more accurate if a quarterback <u>plants</u> his feet and then throws the ball to the receiver.

    c. The <u>plants</u> on the west side of town are closing and being torn down for a new housing development.

    d. Every year my neighborhood <u>plants</u> a community garden.

10. Using information from the fourth paragraph, which of the following statements **might** be true?

    a. The closer a galaxy is to the Milky Way galaxy, the smaller it is.

    b. Gravity keeps the smaller galaxies in orbit around the Milky Way.

    c. The Andromeda galaxy is the largest galaxy in space.

    d. Dwarf galaxies may one day invade the Milky Way galaxy.

11. What does the Hubble Space Telescope use to cut through dust and light in space so that scientists can view the manufacturing of stars?

    a. a magnifying glass

    b. a laser beam

    c. an infrared camera

    d. a powerful spotlight

Part B - Bonus Review

Here is an **idiom**: "The pot calling the kettle black."

People used to do their cooking over an open fire. The pots and pans and kettles they used for cooking would turn black from the fire's smoke. It is ridiculous to "accuse" a kettle of being black because the pot is also black. If I am very stingy and I accuse you of being very stingy, that is a lot like a pot calling a kettle black.

Anaphora means "a pronoun or other words used to refer to some other word or name." Pronouns are one type of **anaphora**.

Lesson 69 Review

Part A - Review

Directions: Read the passage below and then answer the questions.

The immune system helps defend the body against diseases and other harmful invaders. The immune system is made up of cells, molecules, and tissues. It provides protection against a variety of substances that may become harmful if they invade the body. Included in this group are disease-causing organisms such as bacteria, fungi, parasites, and viruses. Our body's ability to resist these invaders is called *immunity*.

A <u>key</u> characteristic of the immune system is its ability to destroy alien invaders while leaving the body's healthy tissues alone. Some white blood cells make special chemicals called antibodies. The process of making antibodies happens very quickly. Within a few days of an invader entering the body, a large number of antibodies have already entered the blood stream searching for the invader.

What happens when the sickness has passed? Most of the antibodies leave the body, but there is a group of white blood cells that remain. They remember how to make the antibody quickly if the virus enters the body again. In the future, the antibodies will destroy the virus before it can do any damage to the body. That's why it's unusual to get diseases like whooping cough and scarlet fever more than once.

If the immune system doesn't work correctly, or breaks down all together, it is known as an immune disorder. One example of an immune disorder is the way the body reacts to pollen or certain foods. An *allergic reaction* to pollen produces antibodies that attack the foreign substance, but often result in a runny nose, sneezing, and red, watery eyes.

If the body has an *autoimmune disorder*, it will produce antibodies that attack the body's own healthy tissues. These diseases are sometimes passed on through family genes. Sometimes they are caused by exposure to certain chemicals. These diseases can also occur after the body has fought off an infection caused by a virus.

If the body's immune system breaks down all together, it is unable to protect itself against any disease. An *immune deficiency disorder* results in the body experiencing repeated infections with no way to fight them off. Some immune deficiencies disorders are inherited, but others are developed during a person's lifetime.

The immune system cannot protect the body from all diseases by itself. Sometimes it needs help. Vaccines boost the body's ability to defend itself against particular types of viruses or bacteria. During the immunization process, physicians give patients vaccines to help protect them from certain severe, life-threatening infections. Kids get their first shots soon after they're born, and then regularly until about age two. They need shots again before they begin kindergarten. Most shots are given by injection with a needle. Because most kids get these shots, diseases like measles, mumps, or polio are rare. These are diseases that used to make many people very sick. Today, some diseases no longer exist just because everyone got their shots!

1. After reading the seventh paragraph of the passage, place an **X** next to the three statements below that are details from the paragraph. Write **MI** next to the statement that is the main idea of the paragraph.

    a. _____ Sometimes the body needs help fighting diseases.

    b. _____ Vaccines help the body fight certain viruses or bacteria.

    c. _____ Shots begin soon after birth.

    d. _____ Because of vaccines, many diseases are rare.

2. Why might a vaccination be seen as a "double-edged sword?"

    _____

    _____

3. Which of the following would be the best title for this passage?

    a. The Body's Army

    b. Wiping Out Disease

    c. A Shot in the Arm

    d. Disorders of the Circulatory System

4. Which of the following questions does the first paragraph answer?

    a. How quickly does the body manufacture antibodies?

    b. What is the difference between a virus and a bacteria?

    c. What is the purpose of the immune system?

    d. Do all animals have immune systems?

5. The author included the third paragraph in order to:

    a. discuss the purpose of red blood cells

    b. explain why it is unusual to get some diseases more than once

    c. repeat an idea that was written about in an earlier paragraph

    d. explain the symptoms of whooping cough and scarlet fever

6. Which one of the following would **not** be considered an immune disorder?

    a. an allergic reaction to pollen

    b. the body's inability to fight off any type of disease

    c. vaccinations that help the body defend itself against disease

    d. antibodies that attack healthy cells

7. Which causes antibodies?

    a. infection

    b. vaccines

    c. deficiencies

    d. red blood cells

8. How would most young children probably feel about vaccines?

    a. fearful

    b. angry

    c. patient

    d. joyous

9. In the second paragraph, the underlined word "<u>key</u>" means:

    a. a low island

    b. basic importance

    c. a musical pitch

    d. a individual part of a computer keyboard

10. Which one of the following produces antibodies?

    a. white blood cells

    b. red blood cells

    c. fungi

    d. tissues

Part B - Bonus Review

Hyperbole is an exaggeration made on purpose. **Hyperbole** is pronounced like this:

    hi PER bow lee

Here is a common example of **hyperbole**: "The new guy on our soccer team is bigger than a truck."

Hyperbole comes from Greek.

A **myth** is a traditional or legendary story. Edgar Allen Poe refers to "Pallas" in "The Raven." Pallas was a goddess of wisdom in Greek **mythology**. **Myth** comes from a Greek word meaning "story."